GARBO ON GARBO

LARGE PRINT

ISIS publish a wide range of books in large print, from fiction to biography. A full list of titles is available free of charge from the address below. Alternatively, contact your local library for details of their collection of ISIS books.

Details of ISIS unabridged audio books are also available.

Any suggestions for books you would like to see in large print or audio are always welcome.

ISIS
55 St Thomas' Street
Oxford OX1 1JG
(0865) 250333

Garbo on Garbo

SVEN BROMAN

ISIS
LARGE PRINT
Oxford, England

FOREWORD

This book is an attempt to provide a few glimpses of Greta Garbo as a person, and of her thoughts and ideas.

I am both pleased and grateful for the active participation of Gunnila Bernadotte in this attempt, which has lent it extra substance. She made more than thirty of Garbo's letters available to me: from her most active period in films in the thirties and from her more silent years in the forties.

Gunnila's parents, Nils and Hörke, the Count and Countess Wachtmeister of Tistad Castle in Södermanland, were very close to Garbo, who was able to rest at Tistad in spring, summer, autumn and winter. It was there that she regained her equilibrium between those stressful periods in Hollywood. This was the place she longed to come back to and it was in Södermanland that she wanted to live.

Sven Broman

1

'I Have Always Needed Someone To Give Me A Push'

'I have never owned a beauty box. When I was making a film, I would use very few cosmetics for my make-up. I used to keep a compact, a lipstick and some cream wrapped in a large handkerchief in my room at the studios.

'I had an offer from Palmolive to advertise their soap for a king's ransom. I declined. After all, I had never used Palmolive. I have always used lavender soap.

'I have never had a face-lift or any kind of operation on my face. I have always kept my own eyelashes.'

'But you did appear in an advertisement for soap at home in Sweden before you went to Hollywood. I have seen one in a minor Swedish film magazine from the early twenties, in which you advertised YvY soap. Your sister did the same kind of thing for YvY.'

'Yes, that's true—it was Alva who had met a fellow from Scania. We were given a whole carton of soap . . . We were both so young and green. It was Swedish soap.'

Garbo would speak only when she wanted to and it was very difficult to steer the conversation. I couldn't do it. I tossed questions at her, some of them fairly easy ones —but she answered only when it suited her. At times she seemed to be wrapped deep in thought about matters I had brought up and then would spontaneously start talking about them the next day.

'There are times when I spend day after day just walking up and down my room talking to myself,' she explained. 'Once the doctor [Dr Jorg Egger in Klosters] was supposed to come and see me. When he heard what sounded like someone talking in my room he thought I had company. He was such a tactful man that he left. But it was only me talking to myself'

Why did Garbo's film career come to such an abrupt and final end so early on? She was only thirty-six in 1941. It was the Second World War. Hollywood's film exports to Europe were in decline. But no other actor of Garbo's status retired. And

Garbo was in demand. There were several film companies interested in her. Apart from Garbo's own, MGM, Paramount made twenty different offers. Fox tried to get her through Darryl F. Zanuck, so did David Selznick, and Jack Warner and many others were keen to hire her.

Two-Faced Woman—Garbo's last film—was something of a disappointment but was not bad at all. Let's just say it was a fairly average picture. You are allowed one of those after a whole series of major hits.

Hollywood supplied the whole world with films. The USA itself was a vast market. But no onc has ever suggested that Garbo was out of work for lack of public interest.

In the summer of 1986— the second year I had the opportunity of meeting Garbo— I put the inevitable question to her: 'Why was it that you stopped filming so abruptly?'

By this time my relations with Garbo had become very positive. She was in good form and more easygoing than usual. I held my breath with excitement when she started to speak: 'I was tired of Hollywood. I did not like my work. There were many days when

I had to force myself to go to the studio. I did not get any good scripts or any good ideas for films. I actually went on filming longer than I had intended. I really wanted to live another life. I wanted to stop earlier but had been bound by the terms of my contract. And my last film was only made so that I could fulfil my contractual commitments.'

'Were you so disappointed with your last film, *Two-Faced Woman*, that you gave it all up because of that?'

'No, that film was hardly any worse than any other but I had started to abandon my film career a long time before that. The movie company, MGM, had a lot of problems with *Two-Faced Woman*. The Catholic Church protested about the film's morality. And Mr Mayer agreed to see a Catholic bishop, who managed to get part of the film cut. I got masses of horrid letters from women's organizations around the USA—I had never had any before. Quite the reverse. You really couldn't take a trivial film like that so seriously

But I have never been a Catholic and never will be.

'The company did everything to make me go on. But I never really felt I wanted to. Mr Mayer courted me zealously but sent such unpleasant people after me: a stupid lawyer in New York and the director he was closest to in Hollywood. Two individuals I could not talk to.'

'But were other movie companies interested?'

'Yes. I got a lot of offers . . . for many years . . . and of course, there were some proposals I did consider. But no one seems to understand that I was tired of everything that had to do with Hollywood. And I was never any real kind of actress, I couldn't go on stage.

'But I still don't understand. Your films were a success the whole world over; it must have been tempting to continue when people idolized you.'

'I always wanted to do my best. I got nothing free, I had to work hard. But I also got pursued and persecuted. I could never be left alone. And I dreamed of being left in peace. I was only a girl when I started, after all. I never thought that I had a childhood like other people. Then there was the press—of which you, Mr Broman, have been a representative—which pursued me and never left me alone. That was no kind of life. It was not worth the price.'

Garbo spoke clearly and matter-of-factly; she didn't seem upset for a moment. I don't think I have ever met anyone who appeared so sincere and frank when speaking about something significant. This made it easy to remember what she said.

'But what if you had been in a position to make your own choices?'

Eventually I was able to decide for myself, I don't blame anyone else. I am just pointing out the circumstances. The war broke out and I felt even more hemmed in than before. Previously I had been able to travel home to Sweden and rest up.

'Not being able to do that any more hit me very hard and I felt sometimes that I had been exiled. But it was the same for a lot of other people and I was not suffering any hardship. And then I have had problems with my health all my life. I felt as though I didn't have any roots.

'This isn't something I want to sit here going over and over again. I do realize now that I was far too sensitive during those first years in Hollywood. Nowadays you could almost fly back and forth between continents every day. It is difficult for young people today to understand how isolated you could feel. Sweden was far away and suddenly impossible to get to. For five whole years.

'Which of your own films do you like the best?'

'*Ninotchka*. I thought it was a true comedy. Thanks to Lubitsch.'

'And yet you made films that have become classics and have been loved by the whole world. Surely that is some consolation?'

'Oh yes, today I really can see that at times I was both difficult and stupid. I regret the way I behaved . . . If I had been able to make some decent films . . . If I had been more in a position to make the important decisions.'

'What were these other films you would like to have made? Can you give us some examples?'

'I have never been prepared to talk about those years and I don't intend to do so now either.'

It was impossible to press Garbo. She was the one who set the pace.

'Did you go and see other people's films?'

'I used to go to the cinema a lot. It was really my only entertainment. It was part of my job to see the kind of things other people were doing. And I also wanted to

7

cheer myself up. I liked Chaplin and I loved Laurel and Hardy. I had two kittens I named Laurel and Hardy. I had a little garden then with flowers growing in it that looked like daisies. The kittens got in there and ate up all the leaves.'

We went out one day for a walk with Garbo, my wife and I. We sat on a bench for a rest, and Garbo said:

'I made my living from looking young. I looked unspoilt. It was really a good thing that I stopped in time. There are a lot of people who go on far too long. I aged quickly. You do that in America. That is why I like being in Klosters, in the mountains. When I breathe this air, I feel that time stands still. It feels as though my strength is returning.'

'But there must have been happy moments in Hollywood as well?'

'I have put that time far behind me now and it feels totally remote from me, up here in the mountains. It is like talking about someone else. It is obvious I was ignorant. Some people have said that I was spoilt very early on. Maybe that is true. But I could not change myself. I dreamed of being able to lead my own life. I had seen so many tragedies in Hollywood as well—it was not just parties. And as I wasn't a real actress, I couldn't just work in a theatre.'

'Yes, but you were a star pupil at the stage school attached to the Royal Dramatic Theatre [in Stockholm]. That must be proof that people believed you were talented.'

'I would never have been able to appear before an audience in my more mature years. I had offers from Broadway and from other sources. One theatre on Broadway offered to take out the first few rows of seats so I wouldn't feel I had people on top of me.

'The stage school was school all the same and that is rather different. It was a good school. Perhaps that was the happiest time of my life. We were taught to speak clearly. Nowadays I sometimes think it is difficult to hear what the actors are saying.'

'One of your friends at stage school [Mimi Pollak] said that you were lacking in self-confidence.'

'That is true. I was totally lacking in self-confidence and would often think that everything would go wrong the next day. But there were several people who understood and helped me. Ernst Lubitsch, for example. He was a good person. He was Jewish and had a strong accent when he talked English.

'When we were working on *Ninotchka* I had something of a breakdown when we were supposed to do a scene in which I had to say some—or so I thought—rude words. I did not feel happy about this and did not believe that it was appropriate to the film we were making. [According to MGM, the line Garbo did not want to utter was: 'Then I will kick you up the arse.']

'I started to cry when the line was kept in the script despite my protests. And I ran off the set quite distraught . . . through the next large studio and into yet another studio, where I hid in tears behind a huge curtain.

'I could hear someone slowly approaching. It was Ernst Lubitsch. He put his arm paternally around my shoulder as I stood there crying: "There, there, my little girl. It'll be all right. Don't cry."

'He was like a loving father to me. That evening Lubitsch telephoned me at home and said that he had reread the film script and decided that I was right. No woman in that role would say such words, he said.

'It made me very happy to be able to work

together with Ernst Lubitsch that one time. So no one should feel they can say that I complained about everything I had to do with Hollywood.

'I was too shy or perhaps too insecure to be able to perform in front of a lot of people. There are whole hordes of people in a film studio who have no reason to be there when shooting starts. It can be difficult concentrating in front of simply anybody.

'But it is true that I did behave badly. Just think, I had two fellows sent off the set of *Ninotchka*. They turned out to be two of the three scriptwriters [Charles Brackett, Billy Wilder and Walter Reisch]. Nowadays I feel ashamed of what I did. It's all the more embarrassing for me since I think that the script for *Ninotchka* was the best one I ever worked with.'

There we were sitting under a blue sky on the path to the Fluela pass at Davos, listening to film history. How typical of Garbo that, in the middle of serious matters, she asked if we had heard the following story:

'There was this fellow who was very drunk but decided to drive his car all the same. A policeman saw him totter into his car and went up to him to make an arrest.

11

But the man had sat down in the back seat. The policeman leant in and asked:

"Are you going to drive?"

"Sure, but someone's stolen the steering wheel." '

Garbo had a gift for switching between being serious and telling jokes that made her seem more human and fun to be with. Sometimes it struck both my wife and me that Garbo had a touch of megalomania. And then she would make a comment that seemed quite the reverse, have a laugh at herself and come back down to earth.

Although Garbo freely admitted that she might have overreacted in the course of her career and had distrusted everything to do with Hollywood, she really did have very good cause on occasion. There were times when negotiations were handled very clumsily on the part of MGM. Garbo used to show letters from MGM to her friend Hörke Wachtmeister at Tistad Castle in Södermanland. And when Garbo spent long periods during the thirties with her friends there, MGM would address their correspondence to: Greta Garbo, c/o Wachtmeister etc. It worked well. A letter dated Los Angeles, 17 February 1938, to Garbo c/o Wachtmeister provides an example of their usual tone. Garbo encouraged Hörke to read it to gain insight into her position:

Count and Countess Wachtmeister
The enclosed letter is a matter of vital interest to Miss G. This is why we have sent the letter to you and we would ask you to forward it to Garbo in person. If you take your friendship with Garbo seriously, you should see that she gets it, even though you know she is unwilling to receive letters in this way.
Please do not return the letter to us but keep it as the only address Garbo has left with us is yours.

When it was an important matter requiring a decision Garbo never hesitated to send a telegram. This particular letter is eight pages long and can be summarized as advising Garbo not to sign a contract of any kind before Louis B. Mayer and MGM have had their say. Above all MGM begged Garbo to watch out for Salka Viertel: 'Do not listen to her, she will only slander MGM etc. Do remember that Mr Mayer only wants what is best for you. Remember what Mr Mayer has often said: We may not agree on every detail, but we have almost always been able to find a compromise and reach agreement in the course of our discussions.'

Then a reckoning is made of everything Mr Mayer has done for Garbo, all that he has spent on various projects and rights acquisitions for films that were never produced but were nevertheless developed only to satisfy her.

With its repetitiveness and its unstinting praise for Louis B. Mayer, the letter seemed somewhat naïve.

'It's quite unnecessary to make a big drama out of my ceasing to make films. Naturally, I haven't been able to avoid reading some of what has been written about me and I suppose that much of it is intended to be kind.

'But I do not particularly like banal love stories turned into films—whether it is me or someone else who figures in them. Ingmar Bergman managed to make films that have to do with the real world. Just imagine if I had ever been able to be involved in something like that.'

'But people have still got to be entertained. Your films are now shown on television throughout the world. This means that there are a great many people who appreciate your films. That must be worth something?'

'I don't think you have understood what I mean, Mr Broman. I have never suggested the most deadly serious of tragedies—there is too much suffering going on all around us—but Hollywood does not stand or fall on account of me. I think they have done very well, all those moguls.'

'But did you want to stop working in Hollywood in order to do something else?'

'No, there wasn't anything I could do. What could I have done?'

'Well, you have expressed views now and again about younger actors. Perhaps you could have been a teacher and helped to develop new ideas . . .'

'I am not up to that. Of course, there are schools and teachers today, and good teachers are needed. I'm just not up to teaching others.

'Why not? You if anyone could be a role model. There must have been many people who wanted to be like Greta Garbo and they would all have listened to you . . .'

'Yes, but what you are saying just proves that I have been unenterprising. I find it difficult getting things started. I think too long

. . . I have always needed someone to give me a push. Frau Graessli [the hotel's proprietor, Lucienne Graessli] asks me what I do in my room all day . . . I lie in my bed looking at the wallpaper, is my answer.

I tried to establish what Garbo thought of her own life—after Hollywood: 'Do you ever look at your old films?'

'Of course, it happens. On television. The sound is not as good on television. They must have spoilt the original sound track.'

We were sitting in the bar in our hotel. I brought up Garbo's first line in her first talkie, *Anna Christie*: ' "Gimme a visky with a ginger ale on the side, and don't be stingy, baby." '

'Can you imagine a more stupid line? Mixing whisky with slush! That is just not the kind of thing one does, Mr Broman.

2

The Most Expensive Autograph In The World

I had been given quite a few bits of good advice about how to behave—if I ever got the chance to meet Greta Garbo. Mostly these concerned the need to avoid certain topics of conversation. Garbo was not, for example, prepared to talk about her films nor about her time in Hollywood. Her childhood and adolescence were never to be touched on. She would make no comment under any circumstances on her private life. And she did not like talking about the people she had known, and even less mentioning any of them. And so on. The only things she was prepared to talk about were antiques and art.

They had also said that Garbo could be very amusing, comical even. But she would only display this side of herself when it suited her. Basically you were not allowed to ask her about anything—if I had rightly understood those with some experience. Garbo had to be given the opportunity to take the initiative herself

You can imagine how incredibly nervous I was sitting there—in just a few minutes I was going to meet Greta Garbo.

'I have never seen you looking so jumpy,' was my wife's acute observation as she sat next to me at the bar of the Hotel Pardenn in Klosters. We were alone in the rustic, half-lit bar. It was 17 July 1985. Garbo had been staying at the hotel for four weeks; my wife and I had been there three days.

Garbo was with an older couple at the hotel and had been eating dinner with them in the dining-room. But she was alone at lunch that day.

When we had finished eating and Garbo was almost alone in the dining-room I went over to her table, bowed and said:

'Would you like us to give your love to Sweden?'

'Oh, you're Swedish, are you?' said Garbo in surprise. 'I have been sitting here looking at you, but there are hardly ever any Swedes here . . .'

Garbo spoke beautiful Swedish quite without any accent.

'Well, we don't want to disturb you . . . I just wanted to say hello and ask you if you wanted to join us for a cup of coffee this afternoon.'

'Thanks but I never drink coffee,' said Garbo.

'A drink, perhaps?' I said. 'I don't know,' she replied. 'Are you staying here at the hotel?'

'Yes,' I said, 'I could leave you my room number.'

And I wrote down my name and room number on a menu and gave it to Garbo. A couple of hours later, at about three, our telephone finally rang.

'Yes, it's me. Perhaps we could meet for a while . . . in the bar . . . at five . . . I haven't been there before . . .'

So there we were, sitting waiting in the bar. In a quarter of an hour it would be five o'clock. My wife had a Campari and soda. I had ordered a vodka Martini. I was sitting there as though I had been turned to stone, looking at the entrance to the bar.

Suddenly Garbo was standing in the doorway. I stood up and could see for myself that she seemed shorter when she walked, bent slightly forward, than she had when sitting in the dining-room. She held a walking-stick for support in her right hand.

'Just think, you're from Sweden. I never meet anyone from Sweden. I can't remember when I last spoke Swedish . . . Do you come from Stockholm?'

'Yes, we live in Stockholm.'

'Oh, how I long to be there . . . but I can't go to Sweden. I don't dare, they just pursue me.

Garbo was not only talkative, she was more easygoing than all the givers of tips and warnings and advice had suggested. Garbo wanted a vodka Martini, too. She took a pack of cigarettes out of her small, simple zip-up handbag and had lit up using a throw-away lighter before I had a chance to offer her a light.

Garbo seemed a bit disappointed with the drink: too much Martini and too little vodka. She mumbled something about their having milder drinking habits in the Alps.

'I can't eat much nowadays, hardly anything at all. But you can't imagine how much I miss Swedish food sometimes— salmon pudding—that was my favourite dish, and stewed bilberries and herrings and schnapps. Does Skåne [a kind of aquavit] still exist? And string beans and waffles with jam. I haven't eaten vegetables for two years. I am not allowed to touch shellfish —no prawns, langoustes or lobster.

'My doctor in New York for thirty years didn't drink or smoke. He was almost ninety when he died. He had a girlfriend even in his later years. Oh yes. No one should think that stops all that early.'

Garbo was both spontaneous and talkative.

'It is so boring for me here. I can't do anything. This is the first time I've ever visited this bar.'

Garbo was wearing pale mauve slacks and a polo-neck sweater in the same colour. Her grey-white hair was neatly combed and her lips were very red with lipstick. She wore no jewellery, not even a necklace. On the ring finger of her left hand she wore an old signet ring made of gold. That was all. She was wearing glasses with a slight blue tint. And she kept another pair of glasses in her handbag.

Garbo wanted another drink and this time I made sure that it was stronger.

'I have one drink a day,' said Garbo. 'At five. But never more. Occasionally I start as early as three o'clock but that doesn't mean I drink any more. I either have scotch or else a vodka Martini. I never drink wine. And I don't like bourbon.'

She apologized for having to go to the dining-room and eat with her party.

'I would much rather be sitting here talking Swedish. It means so much to me, being able to feel Swedish. I never get the chance in New York. And you must tell me all about the king and his lovely queen.'

We sat at the bar for a couple of hours until the dining-room opened and Garbo had to rejoin her friends from New York. That was the beginning of an acquaintance with Garbo that would come to be, if not deep, at least lively and sometimes surprising.

You can never make any of the decisions with Garbo, I had been told. And that was true to the extent that Garbo always wanted to ring the next day and make her final decision known. I did not see this as shilly-shallying but in many ways as a form of consideration, a desire not to delude anyone 'What if I get sick and— can't come? . . . Best to have a way out in case . . .'

Garbo rang shortly after nine the next morning.

'Are you still planning a car trip?'

'Of course.'

'Well, then I'd like to come along if I may.'

I would come to learn that when Garbo quietly announced those affirmative decisions of hers it would only be a few minutes before she would be knocking on our door. She must have been sitting, dressed and ready to go when she telephoned.

We were planning to travel by car from Klosters to Davos and take a walk around Lake Davos. On the way from our room to the lift, Garbo discovered a breakfast tray that had been finished with and left on a chair outside one of the doors. She bent down and took a couple of rolls, which she wrapped up in a paper napkin.

'I am always on the look-out for bread to feed to the squirrels.'

In one of the wooded areas along the shores of Lake Davos there is a special spot for birds and squirrels where they get fed by many a passer-by. This was where Garbo would dispose of the bread she had taken.

On the road from Klosters to Davos— uphill for seven kilometres—Garbo pointed out the paths and walkways she had wandered along over the years. A couple of times she had walked through the forest, following a stream, all the way up to Davos.

'I have walked most of the paths in this area and I have almost always done it alone. I am a recluse. Last year I had a fall and broke one of my wrists. I was lucky enough to be close by a cottage where an elderly woman just happened to be looking out and she found me straight away. She rang the doctor and it was only seven minutes before he arrived. They're specialists at broken arms and legs, the doctors here in the Alps. And the doctor wrapped my hand in a plastic bag he had with him.'

We were driving through a breathtaking Alpine landscape with a lot of traffic going in both directions.

'I have spent the summers here for almost thirty years, sometimes right up to the beginning of October,' Garbo said. 'I can't stand air-conditioning and I can't bear the humid heat of August in New York.'

Garbo was sitting in the front seat. She would turn this way and that, struggle with the safety belt. She would point things out and light her cigarettes. Garbo was a sur-

24

prisingly lively person. She was seventy-nine and would soon be eighty, and on the surface seemed fit. When I told her that I had chronic bronchitis, like her, I had to list all the medicines and the remedies I had tried. I took up the cudgels in favour of inhalation. (That afternoon, I discovered, she contacted a doctor in Klosters and started inhaling the next day.)

And so we arrived at Lake Davos and drove to a small parking spot in a forest clearing. I was still absolutely thrilled to be out driving with Greta Garbo. By now she knew who I was— a retired journalist. I put particular emphasis on the word 'retired' and she also knew that I had helped to write a book about her together with Frederick Sands some years ago.

She still asked very few questions. She mostly just joked. 'Journalists are what I can't stand most. The newspapers are just full of lies.'

As soon as I asked anything she was on her guard.

Garbo felt lonely—and said so, too. In the course of the walk down to Lake Davos we sat down for a moment in front of a stone wall surrounding a villa.

'Look, isn't that Greta Garbo?' we heard

a woman burst out in the garden.

Garbo immediately stood up and we went on walking. She didn't say a word.

The walk around Lake Davos comes close to the ideal. In the sunshine and with a slight breeze, the tiny sailing boats with their different coloured sails made a wonderful sight. We came across walkers in various forms of Tyrolean garb, but only the odd person would recognize Garbo. The local people are very discreet. Garbo, like other celebrities, was left in peace. 'It's people like Garbo and other tourists from whom we earn our living,' a Swiss told me.

'What's that building on the other side of the lake?' Garbo asked.

'It's a school,' I was able to tell her, having skied in that particular area for quite a few winters.

'I've had far too little schooling,' Garbo sighed. 'That's why I don't know anything.'

I objected that Garbo was proof that you could learn a lot in the course of your life without going to school. But it did not help: her lack of education seemed to be some kind of complex that Garbo had. She would return to it every now and then:

'I've got my own way of speaking languages. I've never had any difficulty in making myself understood in German, but I don't speak it correctly.'

'I don't have your experience with German, but your Swedish is perfect, your vocabulary is impressive and your speech is refined. So I'm convinced you must have a talent for languages.'

'When I arrived in America, I couldn't speak any English. Moje [Mauritz Stiller] didn't either. We stayed for ages at a hotel [the Commodore Hotel] in New York. I was able to borrow a dictionary, a Swedish-English one, from a Swedish waiter at the hotel. In the beginning I found it difficult dealing with even the simplest matters, like making myself understood on the telephone.'

Garbo would often return to her regret at only having had a few years at school.

'When I arrived in America, I really didn't know anything about the country. My mother had a relative who emigrated to America and sometimes sent letters. And according to mother he had described America as a prosperous country. I don't know where he lived but in my ignorance I thought that New York would look like San Remo with floral displays and lovely trees. But there wasn't even one single green twig outside the hotel we stayed in in Manhattan. I was terribly disappointed. I really didn't know anything.'

Garbo was very noticeable because she wore a conical Italian straw hat that made her look like a coolie.

'Naturally people think that I don't dare to show myself that I'm just putting on airs. But I need a hat like this to protect my face. I had an operation for skin cancer on my nose. The doctor said I mustn't let myself get sunburnt. I've never liked sunbathing anyway and I've no desire to be brown. President Reagan seems to have the same problem as me. He also had an operation on his face for skin cancer, I read somewhere.'

On many occasions the same thing would happen: we would be sitting in silence or just walking. Then suddenly Garbo would say something. It was as though she wanted to unburden herself of the thoughts whirling inside her head.

We reached the part of the forest walk where the squirrels, and quite a few woodland birds, were gathered. Garbo took out the rolls and we discovered that she had also brought some bread with her from her own breakfast tray. A magpie hopped up on to her arm and ate directly from her hand. It was a strange sight seeing Garbo happy among all the animals, the squirrels leaping up to get her bits of bread. All the tiredness had gone from her face.

Garbo took the lead during our walk. She was the one who knew the paths. Every now and then we would sit on a bench and catch our breath. Proudly she showed us her walking-stick made of oak. On its curve there was a little case with a pencil stuck inside. It had a little silver plate with the initials 'E. R. R.'

'This walking-stick is over one hundred years old. It was a gift from the Rothschild family.'

Garbo occasionally wanted a cigarette. She smoked rather peculiar, narrow, cigar-like cigarettes that could not be bought in Switzerland and that she had brought with her from New York—Sherman's Cigarillos. She would sometimes smoke the short, thin Indian cigarettes you can buy in Switzerland (and Sweden).

'Once, when I had been admitted to New York Hospital, I smoked these cigarettes with dire results—the staff thought I was smoking hash. One of the nurses said to my niece, who was visiting me at the hospital:

"What a pity she takes drugs . . ." I actually smoked those small cigarettes because I thought they were less harmful than the ordinary ones.

Our walks used to put Garbo in a good mood.

'I can't understand why people here in the Alps walk around in those short leather trousers. I was given a very fine pair of short trousers—well, really a whole Tyrolean costume—many years ago. I sneaked out on one occasion in that get-up and not a soul recognized me. But I got sores on my thigh-bones from the trousers. And I can't yodel either . . .'

On the other hand Garbo had what might seem a rather peculiar tendency to holler suddenly when we were out walking. It was a sort of faint hooting, to help her get more air. She was entirely unaffected by her surroundings. Garbo was no shrinking violet.

Garbo was always well-dressed. Always in slacks.

'I have brought sixteen pairs of slacks with me from New York. Not a single dress and not one skirt.'

Garbo was entirely consistent when it came to slacks. Once, when she was a guest of Einar Nerman and his family at their house on the island of Lidingö after the war, she gave Anita, one of the daughters, two hundred kronor to buy some material at Nordiska Kompaniet (the Harrods of Stockholm) to make herself two pairs of pyjamas with long trousers.

Our walks did Garbo good. We were very pleased that she always wanted to sit in the bar at the hotel on the days we had been out walking. Quite by chance I happened to tell her the story of an episode from my childhood, and this was fortunate for me since Garbo began to open out more.

I touched a chord I had never intended to. I told Garbo that when my father died when I was nine, the family were very hard up and I had to try to help feed the family in my own small way. We had a wholesaler next to our house and I used to buy piles of writing-cases—bundled inside were writing paper and envelopes. On the covers were portraits of film stars: Tom Mix, Joan Crawford, Douglas Fairbanks, Greta Garbo and others. I used to go around selling these writing-cases to the local farms.

'The cover picture that sold best was a photo of you in a beret,' I told Garbo.

'So you were even earning money off me

as a child, Mr Broman,' she said with a laugh.

'Yes, that's right. It was a serious business for me. And I was happy your picture sold so well, because people in Kramfors didn't write many letters and you had to find something extra to get rid of the goods.'

Garbo would return jokingly to the theme of my having made money off her as a child, in various situations.

'The beret is something people connect with you very much.'

'I never liked berets', replied Garbo. 'And when I got the chance to have a look round the world, I discovered that in France it is the old men who go around in berets . . .'

'But you set the fashion for the beret at the right time . . . along with a lot of other things.'

'Yes, what I am proud of in that line is the polo-neck sweater. I was actually one of the first women to wear a polo-neck sweater and that may have led other women to be interested. Katharine Hepburn also helped to launch polo-neck sweaters for women.

'I have always liked wearing clothes up to my throat. That is where I think men are cleverer than women. [Gilbert] Adrian, who made many of the clothes I wore in films, understood my wishes. And he went to great lengths to help me avoid anything too low-cut.

'Perhaps I am most pleased at having fought for the right for women to wear trousers. For everyday wear and for outdoors trousers can be a healthy alternative. A female shop-assistant at the grocery store in New York where I usually shop used to complain that she had got something wrong with her lower regions from standing leaning against a freezer counter all day long. I recommended that she change to trousers and wear something warm underneath them. She did as I suggested and she got well. She thanked me for the advice, which pleased me a lot.

'But it was really very amusing to hear that my beret helped you sell your writing paper, Mr Broman.'

This episode helped Garbo to open up about her own childhood.

'I wasn't nearly as successful as you,' she retorted. 'But as a child I did try and sell *Stridsropet* [*Battle Cry*, a Salvation Army newspaper]. There were several of us children who used to visit the Salvation Army on the South Island of Stockholm—that's where I did my first performing and singing. This led to my being invited to sell *Stridsropet*. It worked to some extent in the building we lived in, but I was never any great shakes as a newspaper-seller. But I still like the Salvation Army. There have been occasions when I've visited the Salvation Army in New York. I very much like their singing and their music.

We toured the local area in the car. Garbo pointed out the sanatorium where Thomas Mann, the German novelist and Nobel laureate, had been treated for tuberculosis. Nowadays, the hospital has been turned into a hotel.

I pointed out a slope where they had filmed parts of a James Bond film with lots of skiing acrobatics. Garbo had never seen James Bond. On the other hand, she waxed lyrical about Michael Jackson in an almost girlishly adoring way.

'He is so handsome and so musical, I never miss seeing him on television if I can help it. What a star he is!'

On one occasion she said, 'I am just an old movie star.'

When I cheerfully insisted that she was hardly 'just anyone' . . . just think how her films were still being shown throughout the world . . . how her name appeared in the newspapers almost every day . . . how much fan mail she got—she would sigh: 'Everyone who's been in films does . . .'

But when we used to meet in the bar after a successful day in the country a more self-possessed Garbo would be on display.

One evening Garbo turned up with a book she had just received with a dedication from one of the guests at the hotel—a well-dressed younger man with a lovely and happy wife and two lively teenage children. One might have guessed that he was a successful businessman but he was in fact a preacher from the USA.

Garbo showed us the book, which consisted of an anthology of religious reflections that the preacher had written. She then pointed out the dedication, written in ink:

To
Greta Garbo
much loved by my mother
and her generation . . .

It obviously offended Garbo, who all but sniffed: 'His mother's generation! You should see the piles of letters I get from young people as well.'

On occasion we were given amusing evidence that Garbo, for all her simplicity and straightforwardness in many situations, was nevertheless in no doubt as to her greatness. One day I showed her a newspaper article about an auction of autographs in New York. The year before, the autograph of the Ayatollah Khomeini had fetched the highest price at this auction, but this year Garbo had regained her top position.

'Your autograph is the most expensive in the world!'

Garbo received the news with pleasure and raised her glass and said in the good old Swedish fashion, '*Skol* to us, Mr Broman.'

The next day, when Garbo walked into the bar, the first thing she said was: 'Well then, I've got my top ranking back on the New York exchange . . . Is my autograph the most expensive in the world?'

Garbo is one of a kind, a totally independent person, as my wife and I would discover every now and then. She fitted in well in an Alpine village, where you get the feeling that the people have got nothing whatever against being on their own and would never be part of the herd.

'I've never minded being on my own,' Garbo said. 'It was my choice. But I do regret now that I didn't live my life differently. The thing I love to see most is an older couple come along the street supporting one another. You don't have to be married, but it means a lot having a partner for life . . . I don't have one . . . I regret that . . .

'For more than thirty years I've been walking in these mountains and I've enjoyed doing it. Two or three times I have been entirely on my own with the conductor of the cable car from Klosters up to Gotschnagrat [a peak of 2285 metres]. I have sat on my own up there and looked out over that incomparable landscape. I've had my own sandwiches with me and I haven't needed to bother anyone.'

Garbo had only ever been in the Alps in the summer. I mentioned that it was at the Gotschnagrat massif that a downhill race had been held for several years in memory of Irwin Shaw, the writer, who lived in Klosters for many years.

'I didn't know that,' said Garbo. 'But I sometimes used to meet Irwin Shaw during the summer. At ten o'clock one morning

I had to go and buy a newspaper at the railway station. There stood Irwin Shaw. He came up to me and even at that early hour you could smell the whisky from quite a distance. He wondered whether we could go to the bar at the Grischuna Hotel and have a drink. I declined.

'I have to be in motion for at least an hour, preferably two, every day. I was a frail child and I have often been ill throughout my life. I think I grew too quickly. When I was fifteen I was taller than all my contemporaries. Walks are good for the head. They put you in a good mood and help you avoid being depressed.'

Garbo's face was lined. Her profile was still classically beautiful, especially when she leant her head back. Her nose was unique in its perfection.

'What incredible eyelashes you've got,' I said.

'There's not much left of them, now. But I have never had to use artificial ones.'

'I can't imagine having such a perfect face . . . do forgive me for looking.'

'It's not that perfect. I had to have an operation on my forehead, here on the hairline, because I had a little bump there.

They did it so badly that it left a mark and I've always had to have my hair combed over the mark on this side . . . and they changed my front teeth in Hollywood, as they were set too wide apart. Now I often have to go to the dentist . . . or rather I ought to go more often.'

It was a mature woman, a mature Garbo, I met—who, when she was in the mood, could respond to impertinent questions as well.

Garbo let slip every now and then little statements of a more philosophical nature. One of the most common was, 'Alas for mankind.' She used to say this at least once a day.

This lament of Garbo's would come in useful when we had to find a present for her on her eightieth birthday. What do you give Greta Garbo as a birthday present? What do you give to someone who has got everything?

'Alas for mankind' is a well-known line spoken by Indra's daughter in Strindberg's *A Dream Play*. We got hold of a copy bound in half calf and wrote some lines with reference to Garbo's—and Strindberg's—lament. Garbo was terribly pleased with the book—so much so that she rang to thank us in Stockholm, which was very unusual, as she said herself.

August Strindberg was one of Garbo's favourite writers and she said she could not imagine a nicer compliment than being compared with Strindberg.

'Well, August Strindberg and I do have one thing in common: neither of us learnt to speak French. Although Strindberg lived in Paris and wrote in French, not everyone understood when he tried to speak the language.

'I know that he courted Sarah Bernhardt and wanted to write plays for her. He was very dismayed when she did not understand what he said and asked him to provide an interpreter. But Strindberg still managed to get Sarah Bernhardt to do a guest performance in Stockholm—in *La Dame aux Camélias* at the Royal Dramatic Theatre. I am going to read *A Dream Play* again now.'

3

'I GET MY LONG EYELASHES FROM MY MOTHER'

Greta Garbo entered the bar of the hotel in Klosters one evening looking unusually mischievous. She clapped her hands and said to my wife and me: 'I really am the strangest person in the world. I was born twice.'

This was Garbo in top form. The background to it all was some newspaper articles in the Swedish press that questioned whether Garbo really was born in Stockholm. According to them she was not: she had been born in a little village in Småland, where her mother came from.

This was in the summer of 1986. It seems to be a characteristic of many historical figures that various sites compete to be their birthplace. The parish of Högsby in Småland, where her mother, Anna Lovisa, was born, congratulated Garbo very warmly on her eightieth birthday in 1985.

41

They sent presents that included a folding teak chair made in the local furniture factory. Garbo picked it up in New York, where she was greatly amused at all the speculation going on about her new birthplace. The truth is that Garbo was born on 18 September 1905 at seven-thirty a.m. in the Södra Maternity Hospital in Stockholm.

We started talking about her mother because she herself brought up the subject of all the speculation about her birthplace. Garbo became very serious at this point.

'I've often wanted to cry when I read the crazy things they write about me, such as my being Daddy's girl and not having had such a close relationship with my mother. It was not like that at all.'

Garbo, just like Ingrid Bergman, was very concerned about her good name in Sweden. It was regrettable if newspapers round the world wrote things about her that were wrong, but it was a catastrophe if lies were published about her in the Swedish press.'

Over and over again she would sigh, 'I don't want Swedes to have to feel ashamed of me.

Garbo's mother was born on 10 September

1872. She moved to Stockholm in 1897, where she met Karl Alfred Gustafsson, whom she married on 8 May 1898. Ten weeks later Sven Gustafsson was born, Garbo's elder brother. Her mother's parents had lived and worked in various places, including Applaryd, Gösebo and Skruv-shult in Småland. One of Garbo's cousins still lives in Virstad.

Despite all the clarification by the authorities in Stockholm, some of the inhabitants of Lillsjödal are unwilling to abandon the idea that Garbo came into the world in Småland. Not only can they name the midwife, one Ida Svensson in Lillsjödal, who was supposed to have helped Garbo's mother with the delivery, but they also insist that Garbo's first baby clothes were made locally, sewn by the seamstress Hulda Svensson. They say that Anna Lovisa stayed on there with her child for a month or two after the birth.

It was Garbo who brought the whole question up and who then totally refuted the idea.

'I was born in Stockholm. And I don't believe in reincarnation either.'

Garbo's mother had five brothers and sisters. Her maternal grandfather was a farmer and a bit of an adventurer. When the sixth child was born he left his family and emigrated to the USA, where he had planned a new and richer life. But his dream went wrong and after a few years he returned to the family in Småland.

'It makes me so upset when I read that I am supposed not to have been close to my mother,' Garbo said. 'I don't understand how people can write so much about something they know nothing about . . . Alva, my sister, and I always called our mother Anna. All three of us were so very close to one another. By the way, I always called my sister Alva, Lillan. She was two years older than me almost to the day.

'I cannot remember my mother ever saying a cross word to me. She was widowed early and her health was poor. I was always worried about her when I was in Hollywood. Like my sister Alva, I get my long eyelashes from my mother. "If you've got long eyelashes, you only have to see what you want to," my mother used to say. She was tolerant by nature. She used to say that you should concern yourself only with what is your business.

'While we were growing up during the First World War, most things were in short supply. Of course, we did live in modest circumstances, but we always had enough food for the day . . . We used to have an allotment in Enskede where Alva and I liked to spend time in the summer. We used to grow carrots and beetroot and potatoes there. We had redcurrant bushes and two raspberry canes. Occasionally we had such a bumper harvest that we were able to sell some of our potatoes. There were lilac bushes growing behind our building on Blekinge Street. I used to love white lilacs and still do.

'My mother was almost always in a good mood. She used to sing as well. I used to love a Salvationist song she taught us and I can still sing it to this day:

> *Why must people fight*
> *why must blood flow . . .*

'I am like my father in one way: he loved walking and he often went for long walks all on his own. My father had a sense of humour and always used to cheer people up. His motto was: "Things will be better tomorrow." But he used to complain sometimes about not having been able to go to school and study.'

Garbo went to the Katarina Elementary School on the South Island of Stockholm for six years. That was all the schooling she received. The last two years the class consisted entirely of girls. Some of them who have stayed in Stockholm still keep in touch and get together now and again. They are all about eighty-five (in 1990) and may well be Garbo's oldest fan club. Hardly any of them have had any contact with Garbo since she stopped going to school. Their classroom teacher, Linnea Rosenqvist, used to gather her pupils together once a year—even after the girls had left school.

The last time Greta attended one of these gatherings was when she was eighteen. As usual, she sat quietly next to a schoolfriend who was just as tall as Garbo, Sonja Eriksson.

'I think I used to sleep much less than other children,' Garbo told me. 'I was out running around far too late in the evenings. It's true that our home was very simple, but I'm sure I never lacked for anything during my school years. All my schoolfriends lived in much the same kind of circumstances. There were no children of the rich on Stockholm's South Island.

'I was also precocious because I grew so

quickly. I almost had a complex about being the tallest in the class and that was the reason I sat furthest back.'

Of the four childhood friends still alive, it was Ebba Antonsson who was closest to Greta the schoolgirl:

'We lived near one another and I spent a lot of time with the Gustafsson family. Greta's father worked nights and slept during the day. Greta and her sister, Alva, slept in the kitchen, while their parents slept in the living-room. Since their father had to sleep during the day we had to be quiet and we mostly kept to the kitchen. I didn't find school as easy as Greta: she seemed never to do any homework but knew all the answers anyway.

'Greta's mother Anna didn't just look after the home. After she was widowed she did several hours cleaning at a local jam factory every day. She also had a paper round early every morning in the area around Blekinge Street. Greta's mother always had freshly baked bread to offer us and we all thought she was lovely.'

'They've written a lot about my working as a child at a barber's shop, lathering the faces of the men to be shaved,' a cheery Garbo said. 'I didn't just work at one barber's but at three—mostly on Göt Street, where they had the most customers. No one forced me to work. I gave my earnings to mother but I spent the tips mostly on chocolate. I even had a regular, a posh gentleman who would come over from Östermalmstorg and would allow only me to lather his face. I used to joke with him sometimes and usually put a dollop of lather on his nose. If I didn't do it, he would say: "Don't forget the tip of my nose."

'I can remember one Swedish American who used to come to be shaved fairly often and whose mouth was full of gold fillings. One day one of his gold fillings had fallen out. "Now you can choose between a gold tooth or 25 öre," he said. I thanked him and took the 25-öre coin, which was more than I usually got.

'It made my mother happy when I got a job at the PUB department store. She used to tell me that she would walk past the store telling herself that her daughters were working inside, "in paradise". Yes, she did—she called PUB "paradise". Only once did my mother come in to have a look at me while I was working.

'I was only a few days from my fifteenth birthday when I started the job at PUB and mother said it was the best birthday present I could get. My future would be assured. I would be able to work at PUB for the rest of my life, which might have been just as well . . .'

It was the manager, Ernst Lundgren, who gave Garbo her job at PUB. He told me: 'I can remember walking past one of the changing rooms where Garbo, then fifteen, was attempting to persuade a customer to buy a dress. She was very persuasive and considerate. "A good sales-girl," I said to myself "She'll go far." '

'It was mother who taught me to be carefull with money,' Garbo told me. 'She really did look after the pennies. She was a bright person. I am not at all sure that my character is as good as hers was. Above all, I'm an insecure person. My mother was shy and retiring—but she was never insecure.

'I really did grow too fast as a child. I was taller than all the other children of my age. I think I reached my full growth as soon as I was fourteen. And then I was a sickly child, as well. My mother used to give me cod-liver oil.

' "You have to get strong," said mother, "so that you won't get Spanish flu." That was a terrible scourge during the First

World War and sent many people to an early grave.

'I was a bit odd as a child: I would never go to bed. As an adult I sleep a lot more and I can't stay up long in the evening. I have actually spent a large part of my life lying in bed. Here at the hotel, too. I can spend whole days in bed without being ill.

'But I do like having a look round together with you both, going up into the mountains in your car. But I have to be with people I get on with.

'I read quite a bit. At home in New York I watch television—but never sport. I lie in bed looking at television. When I'm in New York I get up and make my own meals. Then I go to bed. I sit in bed and eat. There really aren't many people who spend as much time in bed as I do.

'I don't watch television here in Switzerland. And now I've got more reasons to want to be lying in bed. My kidney problems make me so tired. Frau Graessli brought a television up to my room when one of my old films was being shown on German television. But the film had been dubbed into German—it wasn't my voice—so I turned it off.'

During the year or so that Garbo worked at PUB various events occurred. Paul U. Bergström—PUB—was the first Swedish business company to make use of filmed advertisements. One of the commercials made in 1920 features a mother and father with their child walking round the department store, buying clothes in the various departments. The child's role was played by a boy whose uncle, Max Gumpel, was a successful construction engineer, a young tycoon from Stockholm's business world.

Gumpel was curious about how shooting a film worked and he visited PUB to see his nephew perform in front of the camera. Instead, Gumpel was fascinated by a young and lovely assistant, Greta Gustafsson. He invited her to dinner at his home and started seeing her now and then. Garbo was fifteen and Gumpel was thirty-one.

'I remember we ate globe artichokes at that first dinner in my home,' Gumpel wrote in a private memoir for his family. This was a totally new dish to Garbo, which she enjoyed very much.

'I was fond of the girl,' wrote Gumpel. 'I made her a present of a gold ring with a small diamond. You couldn't help but see that she was absolutely thrilled. She even went so far as to flatter me that the small stone shone like a diamond in England's Crown Jewels.

'After a year or so we parted like the good friends we had always been. I went off to get married to someone else and she went to study at the Royal Dramatic Theatre—and then went on to be the great star "she was meant to be".'

What Gumpel does not mention in his private memoir was that he was the first man in Garbo's life.

'Greta told me about it in confidence,' said Vera Schmiterlöw, a fellow student with Greta at stage school.

'Gumpel lived at 73C Drottning Street. Greta was secretive about Gumpel but she bubbled over with enthusiasm when she described Gumpel's bathroom:

"I really thought the handles in the bathroom were made of gold and the bathtub was just a dream. He filled the tub up and had a kind of liquid soap that made bubbles on top of the water. I've never experienced anything so nice."

'We ended up being good friends, partly because I was poor despite coming from an aristocratic family. My mother was on her own and had to keep herself by letting rooms. That's why I was the only student at the stage school who spent time with Greta in the summer. We used to visit one another's homes as well. Greta had no need to feel embarrassed in front of me, because I was just as hard up as she was.'

Later on Garbo wanted Vera Schmiterlöw to come over to Hollywood. They were such good friends that they kept in touch almost all their lives. Vera ended up making a career in films in Germany, where, as in Austria, she became quite a star.

Max Gumpel came to be something of a leading figure in 'Swinging Stockholm' as well as being a successful building contractor and industrialist. Gumpel would put flats and houses at Garbo's disposal whenever she visited Stockholm in the years that followed. And Garbo came to be good friends with his family and all the children.

Gumpel, who was twice married, died in 1965. The rings Garbo was given by Max Gumpel—she was actually given two identical gold rings—were the ones she was wearing when she started at the Royal Dramatic Theatre stage school on her seventeenth birthday.

There were six of us who got places out

of the fifty who were tested, including Greta and myself,' said Mimi Pollak. 'We were very surprised that the poorest girl in the class should have two diamond rings.

'I was living in digs then in a room on the top floor. The entrance to the building was from Birger Jarl's Passage. My landlady was a snooty woman from Östermalm who wore a pearl necklace and had the cheek to say to me: "You're welcome to receive Mona Mårtenson in your room, but I would prefer you not to have Greta Gustafsson from the South Island here . . ."

'Greta had a simple coat and an old hat. It was not good enough.

'Among the qualities I most admired in Greta were her persistence and her stamina. Stiller ordered her to diet. She did it with great determination.

'Vera Schmiterlöw wrote to me—while I was at the theatre in Helsingborg for a bit: "Mimi—Greta and I are taking Turkish baths together, partly to diet. I'm not getting anywhere. I've actually put on nine pounds. But Greta just gets thinner and thinner. You can't see her breasts any more. They're just two buttons." '

'One of the happiest days in my life was when I got my first real film pay—for my role in *The Story of Gösta Berling,*' Garbo told me. 'The first thing I did was buy a pearl necklace and a ring for my mother.'

While Garbo had been growing up, the Gustafsson family had never been able to afford a telephone. In 1926 Mrs Gustafsson got one for the first time.

That year, Alva, the elder daughter, died from cancer of the lymphatic glands. The eldest child, their brother Sven, had got his own home. Now that her mother was all on her own, Garbo wanted her to have a better home and one that was easier to manage.

Her mother was reluctant and totally refused to move from the part of the city where her friends lived. She did not feel she would be able to fit in to a posher area. But she did accept a one-bedroom flat with a large kitchen and a balcony in a brighter part of the South Island. And her name was in the telephone directory as Mrs Anna Gustafsson, Ring Street 155, tel: South Island 10586.

Despite the distance separating them, Anna kept in close touch with Greta, who had gone to the USA in 1925. They wrote letters to one another. Anna cut out articles that mentioned Greta in the Swedish press and sent them to Hollywood. And Greta sent home cuttings from American papers and photographs she got from MGM.

A lady journalist from *Vecko-Journalen* (a Swedish woman's weekly) managed to call on Anna Gustafsson in her new flat in the autumn of 1928:

'There was a framed photograph of her husband, who had died young. And there was a photo, too, of Alva, who died in 1926. But there was no picture of Greta, her daughter . . .

' "I've got one here," said Anna Gustafsson, holding up a locket round her neck with a photograph of Greta, a present from her daughter in Hollywood.

' "And I've got more pictures in here," added the proud mother, pulling out a desk drawer stuffed with piles of stills that Garbo had sent home from her films. She did not dare put them on display—"Greta wouldn't like it . . ." '

The interview was published shortly before Garbo's first return home at Christmas 1928. Her mother received the journalist in a spotlessly tidy little flat.

'People think that Greta just rakes in the

money, but she has a lot of expenses in America. Strangers come to me and tell me that their general store or their cafe has gone bust and they would like a hand-out to start afresh. Greta Garbo must be a millionaire, they say. They don't understand that it costs an awful lot living out there.'

'Isn't Garbo going to get married soon?'

'No, Greta has made it very clear she won't. She hasn't got the time or the inclination. She never wants to get married. She even wrote that to me—mind you, it could be an exaggeration . . .'

Her mother would have loved to see Greta have her own family.

'Yes, I do go and see Greta in the films. I went to the première of *Anna Karenina*. As someone who knows Greta very well, I could tell she was giving her utmost.'

'So you were pleased with your daughter then, Mrs Gustafsson?'

'Yes, of course, I'm pleased. Mind you, they didn't need to do all that kissing . . .'

The whole time she was in Hollywood, Garbo longed for a home of her own, preferably in Sweden. In 1937 she bought a manor house called Hårby Manor in lovely surroundings by Lake Sillen in the county of Södermanland, about sixty miles south of Stockholm. Her good friends at Tistad Castle, the Count and Countess Wachtmeister, helped her to find the place.

At Garbo's request her brother Sven Gustafsson and his wife and daughter moved in to look after the land that belonged to the property. He also brought their mother Anna with him.

'She was almost in shock, our mother, at moving from her little flat to a huge house, but she loved being in the country,' said Garbo. 'What was sad was that she had more and more trouble with her rheumatic aches and pains. She was almost disabled sometimes.'

There is plenty of testimony to the fact that Garbo was very attentive and took very good care of her mother during the short time she was at Hårby Manor. She wrapped scarves round her mother's legs and bundled her up in rugs to keep her warm.

When war came in 1939 Garbo was more worried than ever about her mother. Would Sweden be drawn into the war—like Denmark, Norway and Finland? Garbo contacted her family and got her brother and his American wife and seven-year-old daughter to bring their mother with them

58

and come over to the USA. Garbo would pay.

She also got in touch with her good friend, the artist Einar Nerman, who wanted to come and work in the USA for different reasons. With Nerman as their guide, the whole family travelled on the Norwegian passenger ship *Stavangerfjord* from Oslo to New York in October 1939.

After a brief stay in New York they continued on to Los Angeles. Anna's condition deteriorated in the hot and humid climate. Her rheumatic problems got worse.

Following a short stay in California, Sven Gustafsson, his mother and his family moved to Santa Fe in New Mexico. The climate there suited Anna better, even though her rheumatism was still troublesome. It was much more difficult getting used to the strange surroundings. She was sixty-six when she left Sweden and could not speak English. But she was very easily pleased and had a good relationship with her son and his family. And Garbo was behind the scenes helping out financially.

Sven Gustafsson remained his mother's favourite and when Garbo presented her mother with a fir coat, her mother rejected it: 'It would have been better if you'd bought something for Sven.'

Despite all their care, Anna Gustafsson's health got steadily worse. According to the parish records, she died in Scarsdale outside New York on 18 October 1944. She was seventy-two.

Dr Burton Lottlin signed the death certificate, citing coronary thrombosis and coronary arteriosclerosis. Anna's body was cremated and her ashes were kept in an urn that her son Sven took home to Sweden when he returned three years later in 1947. Her ashes now rest in the Gustafsson family grave at the Södra Skogskyrkogården cemetery in Stockholm, together with those of her husband Karl and her daughter Alva.

Sven Gustafsson died in 1967 and was buried in Santa Fe.

4

'DON'T ARGUE—DO AS YOU'RE TOLD'

One evening in Klosters when the atmosphere felt right, I felt bold enough to ask Garbo:

'Which film director meant most to you?'

She leant back, became serious and with great conviction said, as though pronouncing an eternal verity: 'There was only one director for me. He was a Swede—it was Moje [Mauritz Stiller].'

Garbo could sometimes put so much emphasis on what she meant to say that you were given the feeling that the matter was closed—that was it.

Mauritz Stiller gave Garbo her first big film role in *Gösta Berlings Saga (The Story of Gösta Berling)* when she was eighteen. He took her to Hollywood. He himself said that Garbo was his creation. Moje—as all his friends called him—taught Garbo the basics of the art of film-making and was her untiring teacher.

Mauritz Stiller's road had been a long one. In 1912 he was invited to direct at Svenska Biografteatern in Stockholm, a film company that had started up in Kristianstad in 1907. It was there that he directed his first film, *När svärmor regerar (When Mother-in-law Rules)*. During the next four years he directed forty films. These were not very long but they were highly dramatic—mainly thrillers and comedies.

He developed a unique way of working and had an extraordinary sense of what the public wanted. Stiller's film version of *Sängen Om Den Eldröda Blomman (The Song of the Crimson Flower)*, based on Johannes Linnakoski's novel, became something of a worldwide success. The film was sold to twenty countries in Europe as well as to others including Cuba and South Africa. It was shown at court in England and Queen Alexandra herself applauded it.

One of the high points of Stiller's work before Garbo was *Erotikon* (1920), based on a theatre play by the Hungarian Ferenc

Herczeg. In this lively and uncomplicated romantic comedy Stiller's inventiveness and generosity—when it came to spending money—came into their own.

The action takes place in luxurious apartments and the most elegant restaurants, and the characters have private planes. Stiller even commissioned a specially choreographed ballet that was performed by the dancers of the Royal Opera House in Stockholm.

It was Stiller's *Erotikon* that was the inspiration for my film comedies, said Ernst Lubitsch. Chaplin also admired *Erotikon*. And Eisenstein, the Russian film genius, was impressed by it. Stiller's response was to christen his French bulldog Charlie after Chaplin.

It is easy to understand why Selma Lagerlöf was interested when Stiller wanted to make a film of *Gösta Berlings Saga*. Stiller had an interesting way of considering the people taking part in his films. (We should remember that these were silent films.) The most important thing for Stiller was that the actors should look like their characters right from the start. And Stiller even gave the roles to complete amateurs, provided their *appearance* was right for the role.

One of the female leads in *Gösta Berlings Saga* is a young Italian noblewoman, Elisabeth Dohna. This role was awarded to Greta Gustafsson, a pupil at the Royal Dramatic Theatre stage school, because she looked Italian, or at least foreign.

'Well, I've never looked typically Swedish,' Garbo said. 'I wasn't a blonde for one thing, which people abroad always expect Swedes to be.'

Stiller took the liberty of tacking a happy ending on to Selma Lagerlöfs colourful novel. The writer accepted his intervention without discussion and was so happy about the film's reception that she wrote a poem for the première in Copenhagen. The Danish critics were enormously enthusiastic and more positive than their Swedish counterparts. The première cinema, the Palace Theatre in Copenhagen, was sold out. The film was a success in Norway too, playing to full houses in Oslo for three weeks. And it was a hit with audiences in Helsinki.

Garbo was to be interviewed for the first time during the shooting of *Gösta Berlings Saga*. Inga Gaate from *Filmjournalen (The Film Journal)* questioned Garbo, who said: 'You mustn't sit there writing down everything I come out with. I'm one of those unthinking people, you see, who speak first and think later.'

'Is filming difficult?'

'Dreadfully. I'm finding it very difficult, but Stiller's the most generous person I know. You don't get either angry or upset however much you get told off. He creates individuals and then shapes them in line with what he wants.

'Otherwise I am a nice, well-behaved girl who gets very upset if people are nasty to me. Of course, you do have to be a bit cheeky sometimes, although it's not very ladylike. It may well be that I don't have too much of that delightful quality.'

Stiller had one quality as a director and boss that Garbo and many of her colleagues worshipped: he was generous with praise and recognition whenever anyone did anything well. He was a far-sighted man and came to play a great part in Garbo's development, in personal terms as well.

'I've always had a complex because I had so little schooling, but Moje always used to discuss it by saying that you could acquire knowledge in many ways. The most important things were experience and openness.'

Stiller himself had only been to elementary school in Finland. His mother committed suicide when he was three and his father died shortly afterwards. The children were looked after by a foster father who had a factory that produced caps in Helsinki. Stiller began working there as a child and his stepfather wanted him to be a travelling salesman in hats and caps.

Stiller's father was a Russian Jew and a regimental musician by trade. At home they spoke Yiddish but at the cap factory, where all the furriers were Russians, he learnt Russian.

As he approached the age for national service, Stiller grew anxious at the prospect of being forced—against his wishes— to go to Russia to do his military service. He obtained a false passport and made his way under the name of Oscar Rydberg via Haparanda to Sweden. His interest in the theatre had already been awakened and he was able to earn his living as a touring actor, mainly in operettas. Mauritz Stiller was a stylish young man with an impressive voice.

It is Garbo's name that has entered posterity's hall of fame and nowadays mention is mostly made of Mauritz Stiller as part of her background. The truth is that

Stiller was one of the great European directors whose fame spread to Hollywood.

Having signed a contract with Louis B. Mayer in Berlin in 1924—to Stiller, the offer was a princely one—he changed his mind and wanted to stay in Europe. He informed Mayer of his wish to be freed from his contract, but Mayer would not accept his decision. Stiller determined to travel to Hollywood alone, without Garbo, and find a way out of the agreement.

Stiller's close friend, the Finn Alma Söderhjelm, wrote about this episode in her memoirs. Alma Söderhjelm was a professor in Åbo but spent a lot of time in Stockholm, where she was a colourful part of cultural life. According to her, Stiller was at her home at 75 Östermalm Street when he telephoned Greta Gustafsson and got her to leave the stage school and switch to making films. There were many telephone conversations that evening. Once Stiller was given a final go-ahead by the management of the stage school as well, he was totally drained and, according to Alma Söderhjelm, said: 'It is a huge responsibility . . . let's hope it works out for the lass.'

And then the young Garbo found out that Stiller had started doubting the wisdom of going to Hollywood and that he was even thinking of going on his own to get out of the contract with MGM.

Greta sought out Alma Söderhjelm and asked her whether Stiller had said anything about going to America.

'I told her in no uncertain terms,' Söderhjelm wrote, 'that Stiller had repeatedly said that he planned to go on his own and only stay there briefly until he could be freed from his contract.

'Garbo was very upset. She asked me to put in a good word for her so that she could still go to America nevertheless. And I did put in a good word for her. Maybe in the end it was to my good offices that she owes what was to become her glittering career.'

When Stiller came home, ill and tired, from Hollywood in 1927, he told Alma Söderhjelm about the start of Garbo's career and about their life over there, and then he said: 'Alma, I'm the one who made her, let me tell you.'

Alma Söderhjelm: 'It was as though he had at last dotted all the "i"s and crossed all the "t"s—now he could die. His own fumbling steps along the way had at least for once resulted in a creation he could see was something great.'

In December 1925 Mauritz Stiller and Greta Garbo arrived in Los Angeles by train via San Francisco. A huge crowd of Swedes had gathered and the welcome was very cordial. Standing there were Anna Q. Nilsson, Warner Oland (alias Werner Ölund from Umeå)—a successful crime-film detective—the artist and interior decorator Erik Stocklassa, with his wife and son and daughter, Wilhelm Stiller, Mauritz's brother, and many other members of the Scandinavian colony.

From MGM came the chief of the publicity department, Pete Smith, and the six-year-old child-star, Frances Muriel Dana, who presented a bouquet of red roses to Mauritz Stiller and Greta Garbo.

That evening there was a welcome dinner at the family home of Erik Stocklassa who had been a close friend of Stiller's in Stockholm. Stocklassa had also played a villain in Stiller's film *Herr Ames Penningar (Mr Arne's Money)*.

'I got to sit on Greta Garbo's lap,' said Puck Stocklassa, who was then three years old. He was Stiller's godson and had been christened Erik Mauritz. When Garbo visited Stockholm at the end of the forties he met her again. With a laugh she said: 'Is this tall fellow the one who used to sit on my lap?'

Puck's older sister, Ingrid Kjellberg, was eleven years old when Garbo arrived. Today she lives on the island of Lidingö and at the age of seventy-seven still works four hours a day at the American Embassy in Stockholm:

'Garbo was devoted to children and used to play with both my brother and me. We lived in French Village opposite Hollywood Bowl. Every Sunday we were invited to dinner with Mauritz Stiller, who had rented a house in Santa Monica. Stiller's housekeeper had the day off then and my mother used to help with the dinner.

'Garbo lived at the Miramar Hotel close by and she came to dinner every Sunday, too. Actually she wasn't allowed to turn up before the rest of us had finished eating, because Stiller had put her on a diet. She couldn't bear to look on while the rest of us were eating, but instead used to walk up and down the beach beside the Pacific Ocean.

'Once we had finished eating, Garbo would arrive and would then be given in accordance with Stiller's strict regimen a plate of spinach with a slice of lemon. This wasn't enough to sate Garbo's appetite, so that once she'd gone home, she sneaked into my mother's kitchen, where my mother took pity on her and gave her two sandwiches to take with her.

'My parents knew Mauritz Stiller very well and we let our flat at 24 Oden Street in Stockholm to him once when we were away for nine months. That was when Stiller had a mistress staying in our flat.

'My father had bought an island from Calle Schewen in Roslagen called Munken, and Stiller used to join my father and Calle Schewen there for fishing trips. Usually Stiller dressed like a toff but out in Roslagen he used to relax and wear casual, everyday clothes like everyone else.

'My mother, Irma Stocklassa, once asked Stiller in Hollywood whether he oughtn't to marry Garbo, since my parents couldn't help seeing how things were.

' "No," Stiller answered, "that wouldn't be right. I'm too old. She shouldn't get married at all. It would be an obstacle to her career. She is going to be the greatest star of them all."

'In the house next door to us in Hollywood lived Adrian, the dress designer who became so important to Garbo. It was my mother who got him together with Garbo.

'When I was eleven I had two girlfriends of the same age. We climbed up on to the roof of our house and could see into Adrian's patio. He was sitting there dressed casually with two male friends reading a paper called *La Vie Parisienne*. We thought it was all very exciting.'

Adrian later married the actress Janet Gaynor.

Irma Stocklassa added:

'Garbo had marvellous skin and lovely eyes. Moje taught her to say "I am a poor Swedish girl" and "God bless America".

'We held a garden party on 14 September 1925 for Erik's birthday. The guests were not only drawn from the Swedish colony but also included a lot of American artists and architects. The atmosphere was marvellous.

'Greta said that the event felt like her own birthday party. She turned twenty, four days later.

'Garbo had lost fourteen kilos before she got to Hollywood. Stiller and Garbo met for dinner every day during that first period. Stiller took great care that Garbo should not eat too much. I honestly felt very sorry for her on a lot of occasions, since she enjoyed life and had a hearty appetite.

'One Sunday while we were making lunch, Garbo whispered to me in confidence that she had met John Gilbert for the first time. They had been rehearsing together at the studio.

' "Well, what did you think of him?" I asked.

' "Ah!" was her only reply. But there was so much feeling in that one little word that I realized that it was love at first sight.

'It may have been Greta's secret love for Gilbert that threw Moje off balance.'

[Mimi Pollak told the author that Garbo in her letters was all a-twitter, wanting Mimi to send over Swedish Christmas presents and decorations for Greta to give Gilbert at Christmas.]

'I can remember Garbo talking about her sister Alva, to whom she was deeply attached. Garbo was tortured by the letters from Sweden telling her she was getting more and more sick until she finally died.'

The previous year (1924) Inga Gaate had interviewed Mauritz Stiller, who said: 'Acting in front of the camera requires calm and concentration above all. You have to be able to relax. Get rid of all those affectations. It is the minor key that carries the day. You have to leave room for people's imagination. The film camera registers everything with such merciless clarity. We really have to leave something for the audience to interpret.

'American actors are enormously skilful. Their training is incredible. Here in Sweden we have a shortage of film talent, especially among the women. The Swedish woman eats too much and takes too little care of herself'

'I was so small when Garbo was there, only three years old, what I remember most is sitting in her lap and her playing with me,' Puck Stocklassa told me.

'Two years later I was run over by a car driven by a woman. I was badly hurt, the wheels ran over my legs and my rib-cage. I lay unconscious for a whole week. My father engaged a lawyer called Cooper to defend me. But the reckless driver was well-off and persuaded our lawyer to accept a very modest sum in reparation. She simply bought our lawyer. The lawyer had a son called Gary. He was just a boy but would later become one of the great Hollywood stars, Gary Cooper.

'The young Gary was so ashamed of his father's behaviour that he came to see me on my sick-bed and to keep me entertained he sat down and drew cowboy pictures which he gave me . . . Garbo came to see me and she looked after me as well.'

Puck Stocklassa is today a successful sculptor in Stockholm. Among his sculptures is *The Free Word*, which stands outside the Bonniers Building on Tors Street in Stockholm, but that childhood car accident has meant that his back is still damaged.

It was very difficult to get Garbo to say anything about that first period in Hollywood. 'I can't remember anything,' was her repeated, defensive answer.

But one unusually windy day beside Lake Davos Garbo suddenly said with a sigh, 'You know, I nearly drowned during those first years in Hollywood. I often used to swim alone in the ocean at Santa Monica. Once I had been swimming far out to sea, when I was sent spinning by a huge breaker, as tall as a building. I hurt myself and got water in my lungs and I almost lost consciousness. Then came a new and even worse breaker . . .

'No one was watching me. It was a miracle that I managed to swim ashore. By then I was so frightened and in such a panic that I just fell down on to the sand. There was still no one there to help me. I just lay there on my stomach, trying to catch my breath with the water breaking over me.

On another occasion she volunteered the following: 'I visited Moje's grave the first few times I was home in Stockholm from America. I bought a flower arrangement shaped like a cross at a florist's and placed it on his grave. The next day when I visited the grave again someone had torn the arrangement apart and thrown the flowers all over the place.

'When I asked someone standing nearby what this meant, he explained—what I in my ignorance had not understood—that the cross is a Christian symbol that has no place in Jewish life. That was why some Orthodox Jew had torn the arrangement apart that I had bought without knowing any better.'

I pointed out to Garbo that Ingrid Bergman's body had been placed in the family grave in the Northern Cemetery not far from the Jewish section. It was Ingrid Bergman herself who decided that part of her ashes should be scattered over the water at Dannholmen outside Fjällbacka, where she had spent many a summer with Lasse Schmidt, the rest being placed in the family grave. Ingrid Bergman's daughter, Pia Lindström, had taken care of all the arrangements.

'Were there any flowers on her grave?' Garbo asked.

'No, not when I saw it,' I answered.

'Well, that's how it is, they forget you so quickly,' Garbo sighed.

'Stiller must have had filming in his blood?' I asked Garbo.

'Moje did have some simple rules he used to preach. He was concerned that I should grow more self-confident:

"Don't take any notice of other people.
Be yourself
Don't try and be like anyone else.
Every person is unique.
Don't try and be like Norma Shearer." '

Garbo knew this catechism by heart and she repeated Stiller's advice with dignity and gravity. Her gaze was directed straight in front of her—as though she were looking into the distance— when she spoke about Mauritz Stiller.

'Norma Shearer was a huge star at MGM and she was married to Irving Thalberg. I liked him. But he died much too early. The best die young . . .'

She used exactly the same words as a sincere commentary during a discussion we had about Olof Palme's murder. (Palme was Prime Minister of Sweden 1982-6.)

Although Stiller found himself immediately on collision course with the management of MGM and virtually got the sack, he still encouraged Garbo: 'Don't argue—do as you're told.'

'And yet what I most remember is Moje warning me and other people not to overact. We were taught just to suggest various emotional states . . . it was the viewer who was to be given the chance to fill it out.

'Many other silent films from Hollywood were very overdramatic, with an exaggerated style of acting that makes people laugh today. Moje was ahead of his time, I think.'

While shooting *Gösta Berlings Saga* Stiller said to Ragnar Hyltén-Cavallius:

'Garbo is so shy, you realize, she's afraid to show what she feels. She's got no technique, you know.

'But every aspect of her is beautiful.

'Her feet, for example, have you noticed them? She has such peculiarly beautiful heels—on a single straight, fine line.

'A rare beauty.

'And she seems so touching: you feel sorry for her.'

Garbo would often lie down on a sofa at the film studios as soon as she stopped working. She was delicate and suffered from anaemia.

Stiller returned home from Hollywood in the spring of 1927 in an appalling state. Nils Edgren wrote in the magazine *Vi* that he had fluid on both lungs. Stiller was admitted to the Red Cross nursing home in the summer of 1928, where they had to remove thirteen of his ribs. The nurses worshipped him. Until he died he remained bright and cheerful.

Victor Sjöström was supposed to deliver a telegram from Greta Garbo—from disciple to master—but by then Stiller was semi-conscious and so feverish that he could not understand the message.

Stiller died on the night of 9 November 1928. He was forty-five. He was buried in the Mosaic chapel at the Northern Cemetery in Stockholm. A string quartet from the China Theatre played works that included Pacius' 'Suomis Sång' ('Suomi's Song'). All of Sweden's theatrical world was gathered there. Alma Söderhjelm read a poem. Victor Sjöström spoke warmly and lovingly but finished by saying, with tears in his eyes, 'No one knew who you were— not even me.'

5

HOW TO GET GARBO IN
A GOOD MOOD?

Despite Garbo's lifelong fear of publicity, one of her best friends in Sweden in earlier years was Lars Saxon, a journalist and the editor of a weekly newspaper. Saxon got to know Greta in the spring of 1924. He came driving down the Strand in Stockholm in his Packard, and in the passenger seats were Inga-Lill Söderman and her fiancé.

'Inga-Lill asked me to stop at the steps of the Royal Dramatic Theatre, where she came across Greta Garbo and Mona Mårtenson. It ended up with the whole lot of us going off to a restaurant near Drottningholm and drinking tea.'

Lars Saxon corresponded frequently with Greta Garbo, visited her in the USA and gave her very real support during those first years. There is no doubt that he was in love with Garbo, but she did nothing to encourage those feelings and instead made it clear to him that she wanted his friendship and nothing else.

When in 1925 Lars wanted to take Greta out to a dinner and dance at the exclusive KAK (the Swedish RAC) club in Stockholm, she suggested Lars should invite her sister Alva instead. Alva accepted and told him that after their father's death Greta had been the head of the family—despite the fact that both Alva and their brother Sven were older.

Lars Saxon was born in 1900, the son of the legendary writer and publisher J. L. Saxon. At the age of seventeen he entered the family firm, the Saxon and Lindström publishing house, where he became the editor of the weekly *Lektyr* (a men's magazine) and later head of *Svensk Damtidning* (a women's magazine).

Saxon suffered from diabetes and died in 1950. A few months before he died he wrote a long article about Garbo in *Svensk Damtidning*. He had not only published articles under Garbo's name in *Lektyr* in 1927 and 1928 but had also published his lively correspondence with her on several occasions.

In January 1927 Saxon travelled to the USA and visited Garbo in Hollywood. He describes how he visited Garbo's mother before he left and how she asked him to take with him for Greta a box of Swedish ginger biscuits and a packet of crispbread. Alva had knitted a pair of gloves for her sister, who had written that it was cold in Hollywood—he took those with him as well.

Earlier, in November 1926, Garbo had written a letter to Lars Saxon, which he had published in *Svensk Damtidning*:

You've no idea how much has been happening since you last heard from me. I've twice turned my back on the studio and gone home. Threats and all, none of it had any effect. I didn't go back until I'd calmed down. I was given a part immediately after the end of my second film. I was so tired and nervous. On top of which it was a 'vamp' part.

I asked if I could get out of it but they said no. I stayed home for over a week and then went back and played it. It was a huge scandal, let me tell you. They think I'm mad. And then there was yet another awful part with one of the worst directors in the world. And so Garbo went home for the second time. That's just not the kind of thing they do here.

But I get so nervous about all these idiotic things I'm supposed to do that I lose my head.

They say they are going to send me back home. Don't know how that will work out. Haven't made an appearance at Metro for over a month. Oh, well.

My second film has just been shown here. Lasse, I have to apologize to everyone for it. Dreadful: the story, Garbo, just absolutely frightful. This is not an exaggeration, I was beneath contempt. And I've only got myself to blame. I was feeling low, tired, I couldn't sleep, everything was crazy, but the basic problem is that I am not really an actress.

You have to adapt to conditions over here and what the public are believed to want. I do hope Stiller, who didn't meet with much kindness at home, will become one of the leaders, if not the leader here. He's under contract to Paramount now. I had to stay with Metro where there isn't anyone who cares about me, more's the pity.

I was wondering, Lasse, whether you who've read so much might know of a book that you think would be suitable to be turned into a film for me . . .

Lars Saxon's response was to recommend books such as *Susan Lenox* by Graham Phillips, *Anna Christie* by Eugene O'Neill as well as Tolstoy's *Resurrection* and *Anna Karenina*. He included a film synopsis and sent the proposal to Garbo: a female office-worker who becomes a soldier in the Salvation Army. Saxon was actually asked by MGM to come over and work on the script but after quite a bit of correspondence the whole thing fizzled out.

On 14 February 1926 the twenty-year-old Garbo wrote to Saxon:

Hotel Miramar, Wilshire Blvd, at the Ocean.
Do you think my handwriting's nice? I can write more prettily but I feel it's so pretentious.
Don't you think I'm right? Ha ha.

Dear Lars,
I only walk down to my postbox about once a month— happened to go down there yesterday and found two letters from you. It's so sweet of you to remember me so often. I'm not worth it. I've been given so much and am so utterly ungrateful. Had a conversation with the boss yes-

terday, he was annoyed with me because he thinks I get needlessly anxious about everything. I couldn't talk to him about it. It was like hitting your head against a brick wall. We're too different . . .

. . . I'm so unhappy, I keep getting these frightening thoughts about the future. Still each to his own, maybe it wouldn't be much fun if everything was easy . . .

. . . It's so sad that so few people understand how to live, that would be an art to be proud of. Of course, what would make me much happier is if I didn't think about Sweden until I could travel and instead tried to arrange something here instead, but if that is not the way you are, you can't really change.

My film's been delayed so it may be starting when you get there. Don't forget to send me the reviews, please. I've just finished my Danish book about Napoleon and am longing desperately for something new. I feel I must end by admitting that I make myself go to sleep at night by thinking about going home.

Lots and lots of love, darling Lars

Greta

During the shooting of *The Temptress*

Garbo received news of her sister Alva's death. Garbo was deeply shocked but was obliged to carry on filming as usual.

She wrote to Lars Saxon:

Miramar, 6-7-26
(Don't forget me.)
I've got so much to thank you for, I don't know where to begin. The incredible flow of books and papers and so many, many lovely letters. I can only send you my very, very warmest thanks . . .

. . . It has made me so unhappy being so far away from my own kin, having to be here without being able to do anything for one's nearest and dearest has been very difficult. I won't tell you what I have been going through but it would have been a relief to me if I had been able to be with the other people affected by the same thing. I have become afraid of life—I've got nothing to complain about—or didn't have before.

I earn my keep, perhaps having to live in a foreign country isn't much fun, but there are many people for whom things are a hundred times worse. I wouldn't have complained before.

I've been given what millions envy me

for but the surprises life holds in store make you afraid. I don't understand and can't learn to understand why God suddenly meant me such harm. It's as though a part of me has been cut away. I've tried to go home but everyone advises me not to. If I were to go now, in one or two months I would have ruined it all for myself. They're much cleverer than I am—they say that I can't think about leaving until I've done three films. But I'll go the first chance I get. It may still be another six months but I have to be able to go then. It will be very sad, strange and wonderful to be able to come home, home again. Is there anything better than having something to long for as long as you're sure you will have it one day . . .

. . . A lot has happened here. Stiller resigned from my film because he felt he couldn't work with the people here. That was a difficult time, too. I was so tired of it all; I had no idea of what to do.

You know these Americans haven't the faintest understanding of Europeans. You know how they are. So both the film and I got a new director. He spent all day asking if I was happy. Given all that's hap-

pened I found it all a bit enervating.
The film's not finished yet. We have got
a break just for a couple of days. Stiller's
going to start working with Pola Negri.
I'm still very lonely, not that I mind, ex-
cept occasionally.

That's enough of my scribblings for
now. I want you just to know how happy
you've been making this lonely little heart
in America for almost a year. Take care.

Greta

The part of the Hotel Miramar in Santa Monica where Garbo stayed during her first years in Hollywood is still standing today. Now the Sheraton Miramar, it has been extended, and has a palm-fringed swimming-pool. The hotel is sometimes used as a set for run-of-the-mill films set in Hawaii, when people are not willing to go to Honolulu because of the expense involved.

When Saxon arrived in the USA in January 1927 he went straight to Los Angeles, where he registered at a modest hotel.

Garbo was staying at the Miramar, where she was helped a lot by a Norwegian woman at reception.

Saxon wrote:

'My first impression of Garbo was that she looked as though her eyes were sore from crying, she looked care-worn. Greta had been Americanized only to the extent that she drove a car. So she had at least been able to put to good use my teaching her to drive before she went to the USA.'

He describes how when Greta tasted the ginger biscuits he brought from home and saw her sister's hand-knitted gloves her feelings got the better of her and she started crying:

'The relationship between Greta and her mother was very close and what gave Greta the greatest pleasure in the money she earned was being able to send money home so that her mother could get a better flat than the one at 32 Blekinge Street.

'When we ate dinner at the Ambassador afterwards Greta surprised me by offering me some genuine Norwegian aquavit that she had managed to obtain on a Norwegian boat. She had brought the crispbread and the ginger biscuits with her to dinner and she nibbled at them to her heart's content.'

Garbo had a very fraught relationship with the management of MGM. She was far from pleased both with the scripts given her and the way the films were put together.

MGM concentrated exclusively on making entertainment films geared to their audience, whereas Garbo had ambitions to work in a more artistic vein.

MGM's management found out that Saxon—one of Garbo's best friends from Sweden—was in town; a person she obviously listened to. Louis B. Mayer; who had a hard time understanding Garbo, invited Saxon to his home in Beverly Hills. Saxon was impressed but assumed that Greta would also be joining them. But he was the only guest.

Mr Mayer, who offered Saxon tea, turned out to be a small, almost bald gentleman whose forceful gestures showed him to be a man used to making decisions. There and then Mayer offered Saxon a position as MGM's Scandinavian head, with the job of looking after the company's publicity, etc. Mayer also wanted advice about Garbo. What should he do to get her in a good mood and how could he keep her? He couldn't begin to understand her.

Saxon politely declined the job offer and explained that he worked for the family firm.

As for Garbo's moods, he recommended

that she should be allowed to travel home to Sweden for Christmas—quite simply, she needed to breathe Swedish air now and then. Saxon was convinced that Garbo would find herself longing to return to the greater opportunities offered her by Hollywood as long as she was given the chance to catch her breath in Sweden every so often. Saxon left Louis B. Mayer with a half-promise that Garbo would be allowed to travel home at Christmas.

When Garbo finally arrived in Sweden for her first visit at Christmas 1928, she rang Saxon from Gothenburg and asked him to look after her mother and drive her by car to Södertälje, where Garbo was headed by train.

Lars Saxon wrote:

'During her visit home in Stockholm Garbo rehearsed with Brunius at Oscar's Theatre in Tolstoy's *Resurrection*, but she felt too nervous about being on stage again and her guest performance was cancelled.

'What did come very close to happening, however, was her appearance as a prima donna in Karl Gerhard's revue. She had a sweet little singing voice and a wealth of humour that only those who knew her more closely had any idea of.'

That Christmas, Garbo also met up with Vera Schmiterlöw, who travelled up from Germany where she had been filming for a year. Garbo was more beautiful than ever, Vera thought, and was as thin as a rake. On the boat home Greta had become acquainted with Prince Sigvard and continued the acquaintance in Stockholm.

'At the Christmas dinner given by Julius Grönlund for actors at the Strand, Greta and I were the guests of honour. Greta's table companion was the Prince, mine was Jacob Wallenberg.

'Greta stayed in Sweden until March 1929. One day as she was taking a walk with Mimi Pollak through Stockholm, she suddenly pulled her hat down and said: "I don't want to see that man walking over there. He was the one who was courting Alva and hit her so hard on the chest it made her ill . . ." '

Saxon adds:

'And so Garbo went back to the movies and the surmise I outlined to Mr Mayer, that she would settle in Hollywood, proved correct.'

Lars Saxon continued to publish articles about Garbo both in *Lektyr* and in *Svensk Damtidning,* including most of the letters

Garbo wrote to him. He also contacted two or three of Garbo's schoolfriends, whose memories of her were published in his paper.

I brought up the subject of Lars Saxon with Garbo in Klosters and she commented that he died young. 'He was only forty-nine.' She always referred to him as 'the writer'.

'Lars Saxon gave me all the books he wrote and sent me a lot of other books as well. I've always liked reading. A little book Saxon wrote was one I found very amusing. It was called *Sällskapsvännen [The Society Friend]*. He described all kinds of social games in the book as well as something called "handkerchief language". Dropping your handkerchief meant "let's get acquainted". Pulling your handkerchief through your hand meant "I hate you".'

'Well then, the first thing I'm going to do is drop my handkerchief on the floor,' I said, and promptly did so.

'It doesn't always work, Mr Broman,' said Garbo.

Lars Saxon was interested in both theatre and film and in 1923 he published a book called *Amatörteater-några vinkar (Amateur Theatre—Some Tips)*. It contains advice about how to use make-up to look like people of other races.

'Wasn't Lars Saxon a newspaperman and didn't he write about you?' I asked Garbo.

'Yes, but he didn't invent things. Anyway, what I've suffered most from are the photographers who have been pursuing me night and day taking photographs of me when I had no desire to be photographed.'

'Saxon did publish the letters you wrote him . . .'

'Well, I never revealed anything confidential in my letters. They were quite harmless.' *In Lektyr* Garbo was to give her version (through Lars Saxon) of how it all began: 'The first thing that happened was that Stiller asked me to come out to Filmstaden [Film City—studios just north of central Stockholm] at Råsunda to do a film test. He told me to lie down on a bed and "pretend to be sick". I was scared and laughed a bit hysterically and kept moving my hands up and down over the sheet. Stiller seemed displeased. And I was certain that I wouldn't have a chance after that. But all I lacked was self-confidence and so I was very thrilled when I was taken on.'

There is no doubt that Lars Saxon was a source of great help to Garbo during that first period in Hollywood.

6

'I'M TIRED OF BEING TIRED'

'What were you doing, Mr Broman, on 28 and 29 June? You didn't answer your telephone although I rang several times from New York . . . I wanted to say thank you for the lovely lilies of the valley.'

It was July 1987. My wife and I had just arrived in Klosters, when Garbo came towards us in the hotel lobby waving her walking-stick at us. She seemed to be in good shape.

At first we had tried sending the lilies of the valley through Interflora but were told that the flowers could not be obtained in New York at that time of year. I contacted SAS about sending a bouquet by air only to be informed that the importing of fruit and flowers into the USA is forbidden.

'Why are lilies of the valley so important when there are so many other kinds of flowers available in New York?' asked Carin

Ygberg at Scandinavian Airlines Systems'
VIP service desk at Arlanda (Stockholm's
main airport). I explained that we wanted
to send a midsummer greeting to Greta
Garbo and lilies of the valley were a special
favourite of hers.

'Oh,' said Carin Ygberg, 'let me make
some inquiries.'

And next day she informed me that she
had received an astonishing reply from
New York. SAS had spoken to customs at
Kennedy Airport and the customs official's
answer had been:

'There's only one person we make excep-
tions for in the USA and that's Greta
Garbo. Bring the flowers to us and we'll let
the consignment through.'

I told all this to Garbo, who was delighted:

'That's how it should be. I'll try and remember that next time I end up standing
in that endless passport queue at the airport.'

This was the obvious moment to ask her
what it felt like to be a real celebrity, to be
one of a kind. Garbo had lived her whole
life like that. Does it ruin you? Don't you
get spoilt?

'This is something I have in common

with many, many other people and if you spend too much time thinking about it, it drives you crazy. You know, I once got a letter addressed to:

Greta Garbo
Switzerland

'And in New York there was a letter to me with the address:

To Greta Garbo
The most beautiful moviestar in the world.

'They hadn't even put "New York" on the envelope.

'I must tell you, though, that I've never bothered with letters like that. When I was in Hollywood, like everyone else I got letters by the sackful. But I don't feel any responsibility for what I never asked for. In some strange way I never felt that any of it was personal. It scared me as well, because there were people who wrote really smutty letters. Obviously I've had to have help with it, to make sure nothing valuable was discarded but I've spent very little time on it myself.

'Naturally I was happy when a teenage girl wrote that she had been about to commit suicide but then she had seen me in *Queen Christina* and that changed her mind.

So she wrote to me to say that it was thanks to me she was alive.

'Fortunately not everyone recognizes me. I was once standing in front of a small shop window on a street in New York, when two Swedish sailors appeared and stood next to me. One of them suddenly said in Swedish: "If only the old girl would move, we could see better."
"The old girl would be delighted to move," I answered in Swedish.

'I thought those boys would sink through the floor.'

'And then I sometimes read those dreadful papers and they always say I look so tired. It's really not difficult to stop yourself laughing in this world we live in. But I'm tired of being tired.'

We were sitting talking in Garbo's room, number 410: a double room on the top storey of the hotel with a balcony and an exceptional view over Klosters, the Alpine peaks and the valleys. The room was quite ordinary: two beds with a telephone table in between. On one of the beds there was newspaper spread out, on top of which was a polo-neck sweater that Garbo had washed herself There was a chest of drawers and a suite comprising a sofa, armchair and another chair. On a bench were Garbo's two brown suitcases with their name-plates clearly displayed:

Mrs Harriet Brown
450 East 52nd Street
NEW YORK, N. Y. 10022

There was a large bouquet of red carnations and gypsophila divided between two vases on the chest of drawers. Wild Alpine flowers filled two other vases.

'I never lock the outer door,' said Garbo. 'That's a security measure. I've an agreement with the hotel so that if I fall and can't get up, they can easily enter the room.

There was always a 'DO NOT DISTURB' sign hanging on the door handle.

One of the greatest celebrities of the century was staying in what was really a very simple hotel room—clean and tidy but with no hint of luxury, really rather Spartan. She stayed here with her door unlocked for two to three months every year.

When we sat in her room, the telephone would often ring and we would get up and offer to leave.

'No, no, do stay,' she waved, 'it's just a friend in New York.'

Garbo kept the conversation fairly brief, although she was friendliness itself. It was a Mr Lombardo who called and she asked him to say hello to his wife for her. Her doctor at the New York Hospital also rang once a day. He was more to the point. When he offered to fly to Switzerland and take Garbo home she absolutely refused. It wasn't that bad, she emphasized to my wife and me. She could always get help. And at Zurich airport she would be conveyed in a wheelchair all the way out to the plane.

A year later, however, when Garbo's health had deteriorated a great deal, this was exactly what happened. Her brother's daughter, Gray Reisfield—'my niece', as Garbo always referred to her, using the English word 'niece'—flew in, followed immediately by her New York doctor. The two of them helped her make the journey home: 'My niece is the only one I can rely on.

Garbo remained something of a mystery even when you met her. It was only very rarely that I heard her use the name Garbo'. There was one occasion when we were out walking, when a curious German with a camera slung across his belly came along and asked her straight out:

'Aren't you Greta Garbo?'

'*Manchmal* [sometimes],' Garbo answered and turned her back.

She was nevertheless more natural than most people, totally without affectation, even. If you looked her in the eyes, it was as though she saw straight through you.

In her hotel room Garbo had a crate full of large bottles of mineral water.

'I have to drink a lot of mineral water to keep my kidneys working.'

Despite all her ailments—'I haven't been able to eat vegetables for the last two years'—Garbo was unusually vital. And she never brought up the subject of illness herself. But once when we were out walking one day and had sat down on a bench, she said with a sigh, 'Did you know that they were forced to amputate a piece of Mr Friedländer's leg, who was here with me last year. And my doctor has mentioned amputating one of my legs if my circulation gets worse. I'll never let them do that. I wonder if they're not trying to frighten me into stopping smoking.'

Garbo was certainly very natural:

'The first time I was home in Sweden on a visit from Hollywood—in 1928—I met Gösta Ekman. It was at the Royal Dramatic Theatre where they were rehearsing a play.

I was sitting in a chair watching them. I hadn't been able to go to the theatre any more than most people, after all. Then Ekman came up to me with his hands outstretched and said: "But you're so ordinary!"

'He obviously expected—which is something I've understood from other people's reactions as well—that I would be some sort of monster.

'I'm a "loner", a solitary person,' she would say every now and then. 'I once met Dag Hammerskjöld in New York. I think he was a "loner", too.'

Occasionally, when she was being mournful, Garbo could appear not to rely on anyone. Everyone expected something from her, she seemed to think. She surely had cause for a certain scepticism towards those around her. But on the other hand she found it difficult to grasp how privileged her position was. She had only to point at something to have it given to her. And if she ever got tired of anyone, it was goodbye to them.

And yet it's difficult to say that Garbo was like this or like that. She would continually surprise you, and would suddenly dispel all the arguments and reasons for your doubts.

I once dared to raise an objection when she was complaining about being persecuted by people and not being left alone:

'Yes, but when you're one of the greatest celebrities of the century, as you are, you have to understand that people notice you and are curious about you as well. You have to put up with it.'

Instead of reacting angrily to my comment, Garbo leant back in her chair and said: 'Yes, you're right . . . Thanks to my playing Queen Christina on film, the whole world knows who she is.'

When on one occasion my wife and I travelled to France from Klosters, Garbo wanted us to ring and let her know that we had arrived. I called her from Cannes on the Riviera, and she complained: 'Imagine being free to travel as you want. I'm sitting here like a prisoner.'

But in Klosters what she had said was: 'I'm not shy. I'm not afraid of strangers. I like talking to people I don't know. But I'm totally uninterested in public life. I'm the exact opposite of you, Mr Broman: I'm not curious at all.'

Ingrid Bergman and Zarah Leander have both described their lives—in interviews and in their memoirs. They have also both, independently of one another, summed up their lives in one sentence: 'I don't regret a single thing I've done.'

In that regard Garbo was quite unlike her peers. Off and on she would return to that old couple helping one another along:

'You don't have to be married to have a good friend as your partner for life.'

There were other occasions when she would say: 'No, there's been no man who got me to the altar, thank God.'

Or in jest:

'There was no one who would have me— I can't cook.'

Laila Gumpel-Nylund, Max Gumpel's daughter, told Ingrid Clairmont in an interview prior to Garbo's sixtieth birthday in 1965: 'When Garbo came to stay with us in Stockholm the standing order was not to bring anyone else home.

'Garbo was always bitter when talking about her life. We could see that she was unhappy. She would often say that she would give anything to be able to live her life again and be independent.

' "Promise me, Laila," Garbo said, "That you will never let money or fame or other people control your life. Get married and have a home and family—or else you'll just end up unhappy like me.' "

Garbo used to play with Gumpel's daughters, Laila and Margareta at 'Baggensnäs', the family's home outside Stockholm. Laila said: 'Garbo was good at the trapeze. But when she missed at tennis, she could get very angry and throw her racket down in the middle of the game.'

The Garbo my wife and I met was often not the slightest bit solemn or care-worn. What she would often make me think of was her long-standing wish to act in comedy.

'Did the idea never come up of your working in one of Chaplin's films?'

'I couldn't have wished for anything better, but Chaplin had his own women.'

'One of your friends from the stage school, Håkan Westergren, whose career was more comedy-oriented, had a favourite story: "Well I never got to be an actor like Lars Hanson, but I did kiss Greta Garbo. A friend and I invited Garbo and Vera Schmiterlöw out to a restaurant on Djurgården when we were all at the stage school. When we finished we ordered a taxi to take the girls home. I arranged it so that I was sitting in the back seat with Garbo and took the opportunity to kiss her."'

'Well, we were just girls then and I think the boys had slipped some spirits in our glasses.'

7

'THEY'RE MARRYING ME FOR THE 759TH TIME'

Practically all her life Garbo felt homesick for Sweden. The Sweden she dreamed of usually took the form of a manor house somewhere in Södermanland. It was her visits to Tistad Castle outside Nyköping, where she stayed with the family of Count Nils Wachtmeister, that lent substance to this dream. She spent long periods there during her visits to Sweden.

Just before her first journey home to Sweden at Christmas 1928, she had described her anxiety about the journey to her friend Mimi Pollak, who recalled:

'I wrote to tell Garbo that Nils and Hörke Wachtmeister would also be travelling on the Christmas boat, having attended the wedding of Folke Bernadotte in the USA in the company of the princes, Gustav Adolf and Sigvard.

'Greta and I were invited to visit the

Wachtmeisters at Tistad for the New Year in 1929. We threw some things into our suitcases and set off. Imagine our surprise—and our embarrassment—when on our arrival the servants started unpacking our suitcases in the rooms we had been given, while we were shown into the drawing-room.

'The staff had carefully unpacked the simple clothes we had hastily thrown together and arranged them neatly in the chests of drawers in our rooms. Our night clothes were laid out on our beds. Greta and I laughed with embarrassment—we'd never experienced anything like it before. But I'll never forget how Greta used to stroke the pieces of silver that were placed here and there throughout the castle. She had never seen anything so beautiful.'

At Tistad Garbo was left in peace. Märtha, the lady of the house—whom everyone called Hörke—became Garbo's best friend. There developed a lively correspondence between Greta and Hörke that was to last for twenty years.

Nils and Hörke's daughter Gunnila, who was born in 1923, grew up in a home where Garbo was a regular and welcome guest. Garbo used to play with Gunnila from when she was about seven and a half years old. They went off together to the farm buildings with their horses, cows, calves, sheep and hens. Garbo used to pet the animals. In Gunnila she found a merry playmate when it came to catching calves that had wandered off.

Ernst Larsson, the driver and farm handyman, was a man of few words, but a cheerful and quick-witted fellow who became Garbo's particular favourite.

All Garbo's letters to Hörke from Hollywood ended with a warm greeting to 'Herr Larsson'. He became a sort of mascot for Garbo in Sweden.

'I was only a child when I got to know Greta Garbo,' says Gunnila Bernadotte. 'She was just "Auntie Greta" to me and was like a member of the family for long periods.'

Garbo had the use of the guest bedroom in one corner of the top floor of the castle. From here she had the most enchanting view, that took in the avenue of lime trees, which was as straight as an arrow and one of the longest in Sweden.

A ladder led up from the attic to a skylight. Garbo loved to lie on the roof and sunbathe.

'On one occasion I was allowed to accompany my mother and Garbo to the cinema in Nyköping,' adds Gunnila Bernadotte. 'It was the première of *Camille*.

'The news quickly got around that Garbo was in town. And when we came out after the performance, there was a whole crowd of children who wanted her autograph.

' "No, you shouldn't be up this late, you should go home and go to bed," Garbo said kindly but firmly to the children. "Autographs are not worth collecting.' "

Garbo never signed autographs for her fans.

Summer and winter, spring and autumn, Garbo was to visit Tistad Castle. She felt at home there. I don't think that anyone would describe Garbo as an open-hearted person, but she would unburden her heart in the company of Hörke and Nils. Together they went skiing in the mountains of Jämtland. They hired 'Ullerässtugan' in Åre from Adrian Florman.

On another occasion they travelled by car via Vörmland to Norway. Garbo was unwilling to reveal her identity by showing her passport at the Norwegian border. Hörke, who had good connections in Nyköping, arranged a false identity card so that Garbo could enter Norway under the name Margareta Gustafsson.

They stayed the night at a hotel in a small town in Gulbrandsdalen. Some people thought they recognized Garbo and out of curiosity booked in at the hotel.

Garbo put her shoes outside her door for them to be cleaned. Once the word California was revealed on the bottom of the shoes, the mystery was resolved—Garbo was unmasked. The news of just who the visiting celebrity was, spread very swiftly. As Garbo and her party left the hotel that morning, half the town was astir outside.

Garbo found any amount of activities at Tistad. She went swimming with Hörke far out to the edge of the open sea. She loved to go skating in the winter. On one occasion the ice was treacherous and both friends landed in the water and arrived home at the castle wet through and miserable.

As a 'thank you' for her visit Garbo would present the family with a table lamp or a crystal vase and several such decorative objects remain as mementoes of Garbo at Tistad today.

Gunnila Bernadotte: 'Garbo once said when she and I were sunbathing—I must

have been about ten or eleven years old—
that I shouldn't start wearing a bra.'

'Brassières are bad for the breasts and
ruin your nipples,' Garbo warned her.

Garbo was very keen on discussing
healthy living, perhaps most of all what to
eat to stay healthy.

Garbo's correspondence with Hörke
must have been unique. She was writing to
a confidante who represented the setting
and the lifestyle that were Garbo's dream.
Gunnila, to whom her mother passed on
these letters, believes that they paint a
warm and human picture of Garbo. In
them Garbo herself reveals the answers to
some of the questions about her character.
Not least important is the fact that she talks
spontaneously about her reactions and her
views. What impresses the reader is how little she was impressed by the superficial
glamour of Hollywood.

'I think it is important to uncover this picture of a warm and lonely person that her
letters to my mother reveal, as a counter-
weight to much of the negative comment
that has been made and to all the absurd
speculation written about Garbo,' Gunnila
says.

'I remember how happy my mother was

when Garbo's letters would arrive from Hollywood and how concerned she was to write to Garbo and to send her articles from newspapers and keep her informed about what was happening.'

In order to understand those parts of Garbo's letters about her tiredness, you have to be aware of the fact that for long periods she suffered repeatedly from inflammation of the ovaries. In addition she suffered from bronchial catarrh. In many of the letters from Hollywood to Hörke, Garbo complains about having to stay in bed. When she had been ill, she would describe herself as having had an attack of 'The Trouble' again.

In October 1937 Garbo wrote:

As usual I've got so incredibly little time. Have been working all of this long time on 'Nap.' [Napoleon film, i.e. *Marie Walewska, or Conquest] and still won't be finished for at least another month.*

In the letter Garbo complains that she is going to miss another Swedish summer yet again:

And then I've been a bit out of sorts . . . I really feel I will have to go and have myself looked at as soon as I've fin-

ished this job. There's just no point in walking around like this only half alive. It may just be a minor matter that can be put right if only I can find the right person. But who is the right person? It is definitely not Cloetta.

Garbo is almost consistently negative in relation to the films she is working on:

I'm afraid that this last film isn't going to be much fun. When Adrian, who does my clothes, read the script he said;

'Who cares about Napoleon!'

And I'm afraid he's right.

As it turned out, neither Adrian nor Garbo were right that time. *Conquest* was a huge success the whole world over and today is considered one of the great classic films.

Garbo adored her fashion designer Adrian, with his centre parting and golfing trousers. Adrian is said to have studied Garbo like a doctor studies X-ray pictures. He dressed her in high necks—Garbo loathed *décolletage*—long sleeves and straight lines. In her view modern fashion lacked style in several respects.

'I can't for the life of me understand how

young people go round in jeans they've worn to bits in order to look tough. We were taught to darn and patch and look after the clothes we had.'

'My mother kept Garbo's letters in a box and passed it on to me,' says Gunnila Bernadotte. 'And I've always thought whenever I've read any of the stupid things that are written about Garbo that it would be a good thing to let her speak for herself'

Just as Horke used to send newspaper clippings from Sweden, so Garbo would enclose articles from papers in Hollywood:

Dear Hörke,

You can imagine how pleased I was to read this letter to the paper. Maybe I do some good after all:

'I want to praise Garbo!

I do not enjoy most films because I am deaf. But the other evening I went to see Anna Karenina *and was captivated and thrilled—despite the fact that I couldn't understand a word. That's how marvellous Garbo is.*

There are people who say she is not really beautiful in the true sense of the word. What do they mean? She radiates beauty. She has such incredibly beautiful eyes.

For someone like me who cannot hear, Garbo's absolutely marvellous: her face speaks, it is as though she were performing in a pantomime. And her face is so expressive. It hardly matters that I cannot hear what she says, since she speaks with her heart and her movements and gestures mean that words become superfluous.
Margaret Kelly
44 Clara Street, San Francisco.'

During the filming of *Queen Christina* Garbo wrote three letters to Hörke in which she complained most forcefully. The film was something of a dream come true for Garbo, who prior to shooting spent several weeks at Tistad, where she read everything she could find about the queen. When she returned to Hollywood she had with her a whole bundle of books about Christina.

Garbo had taken for granted that the film would, to some extent at least, follow the historical course of events. The film had been Salka Viertel's idea and MGM had given her the task of drawing up the original script proposal.

Garbo's popularity was at its height and she had film offers from a number of companies in Hollywood. She readily signed

MGM's new contract proposal. That was when Garbo became the highest-paid woman in the USA.

Soon, however, the problems began. Queen Christina was, of course, an historic figure in Sweden, the queen who managed to negotiate a peace treaty with the European powers, dressed in men's clothes and abdicated at the age of twenty-seven to go to Italy and become a Catholic.

But MGM had very different notions of an historical film. A real love story was an absolute requirement. The discussions were heated, but Irving Thalberg, the producer, would not give way on this point.

Thanks to Garbo, MGM gave Salka Viertel, an unemployed Jewish actress who was born in Galicia in Poland, a job as a scriptwriter. This was to be the start of a lifelong friendship.

The run-up to the film was to prove highly dramatic. Salka Viertel was hired at a weekly wage and was to be assisted by various people as well as other scriptwriters. These included Paul Bern, an arrogant and haughty little gentleman, who was married to the platinum blonde Jean Harlow and was part of the team that were developing the script. While work was going on on the script, Paul Bern was found dead. He had committed suicide.

A new writer was hired, Ernest Vajda, a Hungarian whose English was dreadful. He changed the script—his idol was Ernst Lubitsch—and the film started to resemble a comedy.

But Salka managed to steer herself safely through the troubles and was promoted to producer's assistant. A visiting British writer, H. M. Harwood, was considered to represent what was 'classy'. He was hired and it was Harwood and Salka Viertel who received the final credit for the script.

The script was ready and approved and filming could begin. Garbo arrived via the Panama Canal on a cargo ship—the *Annie Johnson*, which could only take four passengers—and was met by Salka Viertel with her car. Garbo had no home of her own and stayed with the Viertel family.

The director of the film turned out to be another European, Rouben Mamoulian, who was born in Tiflis in Armenia. He was very much influenced by Russian theatre.

At first it was intended that Laurence Olivier should play opposite Garbo. She had chosen him herself, having seen a number of his screen tests. But the chemistry was not there. Garbo realized immediately that she would not be able to play love scenes with the Englishman. At Garbo's own suggestion they chose instead her old friend and sometime lover, John Gilbert.

Garbo wrote two letters to Tistad about work on the film in the summer of 1933:

I have been and still am suffering the most sleepless anxious period I've had for ages. I hope to God that the worst is over. I have just moved into a house, and hope I will get a bit of peace behind my closed gates. Marvellous, 'wild' garden— it's huge. The only thing worthwhile here.

There are chickens as well.

God help me if Hollywood finds out that I am a farmer. I have been struggling mightily with Christina, *but the worst is yet to come . . .*

. . . I am so off balance that I can't tell you anything, so no more news than my new address:

1201 San Vincent Boulevard
Santa Monica, California, USA
My name is Viertel.
I don't want anyone to find out where I live, so if you just put Viertel and the address on the envelope I'll get it. It will

*be a miracle if I don't end up a criminal.
I soon won't know what my own name
is.*

A few weeks later Garbo wrote:

*God, I have thought so often about you
all and everything to do with Tistad.
When I got your letter about the summer
there, it made me ache . . .
. . . It's been a difficult time, it all went
wrong. I'm half-done with* Christina *now
and half done is what she's going to be
when she's finished.*

Garbo goes on to pour out her com-
plaints about the making of the film:

*It's impossible to try and achieve any-
thing out of the ordinary here. This is the
last time I'm going to try . . .
. . . If only those who dream about Hollywood knew how difficult it all is—but the
end result seems to be the only thing that
counts .
. . . I long to get away—the Wandering
Jew in me longs to get away, far away. I
feel I've almost never been as tired as I
am now . . .*

The only thing I want right now is to have my head shaved and go skating on Lake Egla. To some extent this might be because I'm having problems with my hair at the moment . . .

. . . Just want to remind you all not to forget me totally . . .

. . . There's the most infernal din outside my room. They're building something or other in the studio—there's so much hammering going on that I don't know whether I'm writing in Swedish or Chinese.

In January 1934 Garbo wrote:

I have been ill and have been in bed for three weeks. I've been feeling so down. Thank you so very much for the little fir tree and its decorations. It was still scenting the air, although it was 'down', too . . . I put it in a dish of water, sat next to it and did a lot of thinking—bitter thoughts and good ones.

You've no idea what it feels like to live in exile and for the sake of 'Mammon'. I suppose I am a true prostitute . . .

. . . By the way, Mammon is taking its time. Christina *took more than eight months. I am so ashamed of* Christina. *I*

often wake up and think with horror about the film coming to Sweden. It's really bad in every respect, but the worst thing is they'll think I don't know any better—just imagine Christina abdicating for the sake of a little Spaniard.

I managed to believe for ages that it would look as though she did it because she was weary of it all and from a boundless desire to be free. But I'm not strong enough to get anything done so I end up being a poor prophet . . .

. . . You know I hardly ever mention my films but I feel I have to prepare you.

At the same time I would like to ask you to do something I've never asked before—would you write to me and tell me what you think when you've seen it . . .

. . . On top of all the other absurdities, they're marrying me for the 759th time. Can you think of anything lower than the people who are in charge of this 'art' I'm part of . . .

. . . They produce the most humiliating articles in all the papers to create publicity for their films. Out of nowhere come long pieces about how I've got married, how I've disappeared, shot myself, gone to the moon, etc. And I never defend my-

self. However, I'm still not engaged, still unmarried, houseless, homeless and love living on pineapples.

Let me tell you what I did on New Year's night. I had my dinner alone in my bedroom (which isn't exactly pretty) with the Christmas tree lit up and thought about my homeland—including all I love.

The above short extracts are from a very long letter—'This has to be the most detailed letter I've ever written.'

It is not hard to understand how Garbo felt. Here she was, all geared up, at last a film she might be able to be proud of And then, as Garbo saw it, a typical Hollywood hotchpotch with no respect for Sweden's history. What would people think? People around the world, however, knew almost nothing about Queen Christina. The film was a hit just as it was. It became one of Garbo's greatest films.

She herself would one day hear Winston Churchill telling her how he would relax now and then by watching *Queen Christina* in his private cinema in his London shelter, while the bombs were falling over London and England.

And when we came to discuss the film with Garbo in Klosters, she was almost proud of her accomplishment.

'Have you seen Liv Ullmann in that more recent English version of *Queen Christina*, Mr Broman?'

No, I'd missed it.

'Well, try and get someone to set up a screening. The film is dreadful.'

Garbo: 'Well, perhaps I did help to make Queen Christina known throughout the world . . . but it was awful seeing what they had done with her remains in Rome . . . put them in one of the walls in St Peter's.'

I was pleased to be able to help correct Garbo's misapprehension:

'Christina is actually buried in a coffin under St Peter's. But at the entrance there is a hugely impressive commemorative plaque—a unique mark of honour.

'Good Lord, so I've spent all my life worrying myself unnecessarily. Thank you so very much, Mr Broman.'

According to Salka Viertel eight different scriptwriters were involved in the work on the script of *Queen Christina*. When Rouben Mamoulian was appointed director the first thing he demanded was 'I've got to make some changes to the Script.' Then, just as filming was about to begin he demanded to speak with Garbo in private: 'I've heard that when an intimate scene is going to be shot in the studio you want everyone to disappear apart from the cinematographer. I've no intention of going to the cafeteria while shooting takes place and I also need certain people around me.'

Garbo answered: 'Well, I agree it's OK for you to remain in the studio.'

In a television programme that Aina Behring, Åke Wihlney and I helped to make about Garbo for her eightieth birthday, we were given the chance to interview Mamoulian about *Queen Christina*. He told the following story:

' "Well, we are supposed to start with a scene in which the queen [Garbo] is sitting in her study. So let's have a rehearsal before we start."

' "Oh no, Mr Mamoulian, I do not rehearse."

'I was very surprised and said that a preliminary rehearsal was very important to me. It improves quality and saves a lot of money.

' "My first take is always the best," insisted Garbo.

' "Well, if that works I'll be the fastest director in Hollywood. We'll finish the film in three weeks . . . But if it doesn't work, can we agree that we will work according to my methods, i.e. rehearsal? I'll rehearse with the others, but not with you."

' "Don't worry," said Garbo.

'Garbo was right,' Mamoulian admitted. 'She really could act. She was an intuitive actress. It was something of a miracle, a divine gift. The point is that with her intuition she was able to capture all sorts of emotional states. You did not have to tell Garbo to look like this or that, for this reason or that. No, you just had to tell her which emotion you wanted to have produced for the scene in question.

' "I understand," said Garbo.

'And she did understand. She produced the emotion on her face, she produced it in her bodily movements—which is more than you can say about many actors. What was absolutely extraordinary about Garbo was that she was both photogenic and intuitive. Garbo was simply unique.'

'Why was John Gilbert chosen to play opposite her in *Queen Christina?*' we asked Mamoulian.

'I first thought of John Barrymore but decided that he was too old. Then we tested Laurence Olivier and both Garbo and I agreed that he was too young. [In fact both Franchot Tone and Nils Asther were also under consideration.]

'Many years later I had lunch with Laurence Olivier in London and he said that he had some sympathy for the decision going against him. After that, there weren't that many to choose from. It had to be John Gilbert. He had problems with his voice, which was very falsetto. But technology can work wonders and I asked Gilbert to speak very quietly. The sound technician then did a superb job. [Garbo on the other hand had the perfect voice for the microphone according to Arthur Wilson, MGM's sound expert: "Her lovely deep vocal range was perfect for sound films."]

'What was miraculous about Garbo was her innate mystique. It is difficult to describe a face of such radiant beauty. I cannot explain a mystique that grabs hold of the viewer's imagination. When an actor or actress walks on stage and you suddenly become aware that the stage has been lit up, that everyone's eyes are fixed on the person in question—that kind of magnetism is nothing short of miraculous.'

During filming John Gilbert became very passionate in a love scene, so passionate that Garbo asked Mamoulian to reshoot the scene, saying: 'Don't forget that Mr Gilbert is now a married man with a wife and children.'

In Klosters I got the opportunity to ask Garbo about another love scene in the film, the classic one where she is lying on her back and Gilbert dangles a bunch of grapes over her face that she slowly nibbles at.

'I did learn one thing,' she said, 'if you're going to eat grapes, you shouldn't be lying on the floor on your back.'

In our television programme about Garbo and her eightieth birthday we gave Rouben Mamoulian the last word on Garbo:

'Congratulations. My love and admiration are always with you. And I think you will live forever.'

When I met Garbo after her birthday I asked her quite without thinking: 'How was your eightieth birthday?'

'That's not what you should say, Mr Broman. You should say, "your day of celebration." Thank you, it was very nice.'

8

'If You're Going To Die On Screen, You've Got To Be Strong And In Good Health'

'Let me tell you, Mr Broman, if you're going to die on screen, you've got to be strong and in good health.'

We were talking about *Camille*. I had been telling Garbo that a Swedish actor friend of mine (Lars Ekborg) had said that the best way to be remembered in a film was to die at the end. 'Then the audience leave wiping away a tear or two with their hankies and you get remembered much more clearly than when it all ends happily ever after,' he said.

'Yes, I agree with that,' said Garbo. 'I've died three times on screen.'

Long before I ever met Garbo, I had become fascinated by the real story behind *Camille*, that is, by the real person on whom

Marguerite Gautier, in the classic novel by Alexandre Dumas fils, is based. The more I found out about her fate—she was called Alphonsine Plessis and came from Normandy—the more it seemed to me that truth outdid fiction.

Almost the first thing I told Garbo was that I had plans to write a book—*The Truth about the Lady of the Camellias*. Would she consider writing a little piece as a foreword to the proposed book?

'Never, ever,' Garbo said. 'I can't write. Why should I?'

Despite that clear rejection, Garbo was nevertheless interested in being shown a glimpse or two of the real Lady of the Camellias.

'I don't think you should be so fond of her, Mr Broman. Just think of what profession she practised.'

I had got to know the last living relative, a farmer's wife in Le Merlerault in Normandy, Mme Eugénie Mariette, who was a direct descendant of the sister of the Lady of the Camellias.

It was in Paris in 1847 that the Lady of the Camellias died. Her only living relative showed me what had come down to her from Alphonsine—a simple pair of earrings, the lizard spine that Dumas wrote about, a necklace and some hairpins.

Alphonsine arrived in Paris in 1838. She was little more than fourteen when her father, an alcoholic pedlar, left her with a distant relative and disappeared. The mother had abandoned the family at an earlier stage.

In Paris the girl had to make her way as best she could, and pretty soon this came to be through prostitution. At first, though, she worked at a laundry. It was when she went to a shop in the rue St Honoré that she met a well-off businessman and became his mistress. He got her a little flat and had it decorated. However, her lover's resources were limited and Alphonsine's appetite grew. Her requirements increased as to clothes and comforts of various kinds. And she changed her name to Marie Duplessis.

She became the mistress of a wealthier man, the Duke de Guiche. Her beaux started to change more and more frequently: counts and barons, dukes and princes.

In addition to her growing demands when it came to comfort and luxury, she had ambitions to improve her cultural education. She hired language tutors and teachers of drawing, music and dance. She also started travelling abroad.

She stayed in Bad Homburg, in Wiesbaden, in Spa, in Baden-Baden and other fashionable spa towns, preferably the ones with casinos and an active social life.

Her apartments grew larger and larger. She acquired servants. She had her own horse and carriage. It was not only her beauty and elegance she had to thank for all this, for she also had the most engaging manner.

Marie was described as slim with slender limbs, brown eyes and black hair. According to her passport her height was 165 cm. Her clothes were simple but extremely elegant and personal in style. The head of the Opera called her the best-dressed woman in Paris. She made an impression not only on the men but also on the women in the great salons.

This was a time in which there was very little of what we would now consider basic social welfare, but charity work was extensive. On one occasion when it proved difficult to get people to lighten their pockets, Marie was invited to participate in a charity fund-raising. And thanks to her the results were a financial success.

Almost every day Marie would visit one of the theatres in Paris. She would always have a bouquet of white camellias in her hand and a camellia on her bosom. It was because she was always adorned in this way that the flower-sellers and doormen at the theatres called her 'the Lady of the Camellias'.

Alexandre Dumas fils was even made a present of the name when he started writing. His novel, *The Lady of the Camellias*, was published in France in 1848. The book is believed to have sold twenty million copies. In 1852 Dumas wrote a play based on the novel. And in 1854 Verdi composed *La Traviata* on the same theme.

Marie had a rule that as soon as she got a new lover she would wear only the dresses and gowns that the new man had paid for. The same thing applied to jewellery. But she saved everything she received from former lovers 'as mementoes'. And she explained: 'I have no desire to appear with one man and have it said by another that "she's wearing what I gave her".'

Marie was really something of a white liar. She tried to make the world look prettier by telling little lies. And when she was found out, she would respond with a smile, 'Lying makes your teeth white.'

What can you say to that?

For more than a year she was courted by Franz Liszt. He moved in circles made up of the nobility, writers and artists as well as prominent actors and singers. Liszt gave his, girlfriend piano lessons all the time. Towards the end of his life the composer said that the Lady of the Camellias had been the great love of his life.

During the cold winter of 1844 the Opera and all the theatres of Paris were closed for seven months because of a cholera epidemic. In the spring of 1845 Marie came down with a serious and apparently fatal bout of pneumonia. Dr David Ferdinand Koreff was introduced to Marie by a friend, Count Horace de Viel-Castel, who later became curator of the Louvre.

Koreff treated Marie throughout her long illness, from March to June. She became well again and was to be grateful to Dr Koreff for the rest of her life. But Marie's health was delicate. Her lungs were not good and she began to cough blood. A new doctor, Dr Chomel, prescribed a diet of bread and vegetable soup. A third doctor recommended grilled meat. Dr Koreff remained in attendance and he recommended quinine enemas and aromatic inhalations. Marie did everything the experts required. She spoke well of everyone, and despite her illness she tried to help the poor.

One of the more absurd ideas for restoring the Lady of the Camellias to health was to drill holes in the floor of her bedroom. This was situated above her stables, which housed two horses. There was a belief that people who lived around horses never got tuberculosis. Marie was therefore to be allowed to smell horses. The idea was rejected, however.

One of the specialists said that she ought to travel to a spa and take the waters at Ems or Spa. She also travelled to Baden-Baden and Wiesbaden. 'They are places along the road to Golgotha,' she said.

Previously another nobleman had provided her with a lovely new apartment at 11 Boulevard de la Madeleine, the present-day number 15, just across the road from the church of the Madeleine.

Thus it was that Marie met her fate in the person of Count Édouard de Perrégaux, a son of the family to whom Napoleon I gave the right to start the Bank of France. He proposed to Marie and against his family's wishes went with his fiancée to London to get married.

In the middle of the nineteenth century, the authorities in London were not very particular when it came to the papers and documents normally required for a wedding. London was a sort of European Reno.

On 21 February 1846 Alphonsine Plessis, spinster, aged twenty-two, was married to the twenty-nine-year-old bachelor Édouard de Perrégaux in Kensington. The poor girl from Normandy was now Countess de Perrégaux.

After a few weeks the nobleman's family in Paris started a cold war against their disobedient son. Édouard was weak, gave in and asked for a divorce. Although Marie had already affixed the family's coat of arms to the doors of her carriage, she made no resistance and let Édouard go his way.

Marie's health had deteriorated and now it would never recover. Tuberculosis made it hard for her to move about. From London she took back with her to France a little English setter called Tom which was totally devoted to her for the remaining years of her life.

Marie could be seen sitting at her window—she had five windows that looked on to the Madeleine church—wrapped in a white dressing gown with her arm around the dog.

Alphonsine Plessis, alias Marie Duplessis, died on 3 February 1847, having just turned twenty-three. She had written a will: everything that was left once the creditors had been satisfied was to go to her niece in Normandy—on the condition that her heir never visited Paris.

The creditors lined up beside Marie's death-bed and an auction was immediately arranged of everything she owned. It lasted three days, writers, artists, the rich and the simply curious all attending. No one could help admiring all the elegant and expensive jewellery and furniture, pictures and clothes. They were exquisite.

The literary critic Jules Janin was there, as well as the Goncourt brothers, Théophile Gautier and many other famous names. Charles Dickens arrived from London for the auction. Eugène Sue tried to lay his hands on the Lady of the Camellias' prayer book. It turned out that Marie had a prayer stool as well and that she had frequently attended mass in the neighbouring Madeleine church. Her famous bed fetched a fabulous sum.

It is to the credit of Édouard de Perrégaux that he did everything he could to ensure that his ex-wife received a dignified burial. At her own request, Marie was buried at sunrise. Her coffin was wreathed in white camellias. It was the Count who had the memorial stone erected above Marie's grave at the entrance to the Montmartre cemetery.

'Apart from the Tomb of the Unknown Soldier, there are supposed to be few graves in Paris where so many flowers are placed all year round. With your film you must have played a huge part in bringing that about,' I put it to Garbo.

'I would really love to see the grave,' she replied. 'You'll have to take me there, Mr Broman. I've never heard any of what you've told me about the Lady of the Camellias before. I read the novel and the film script.'

'In my opinion *Camille* is one of your best films. Dumas' novel is supposed to have been filmed twenty-six times—the first time was in Denmark in 1926.'

'One of the people who wrote to me about both *Camille* and *Queen Christina* was Mao's wife—Chiang Ch'ing. She wrote a very kind letter and said that she had seen *Camille* so many times that their copy of the film was worn out. She had her own cinema.

'Yes, and then MGM has a copy of the letter you received from the daughter of Alexandre Dumas fils. She praised your part in *Camille* and thought your performance was better than that of both Sarah Bernhardt and Eleonora Duse—she had seen them both. "And just imagine how my father would have loved your film," she wrote.'

'Yes, I've still got that letter. It is one of the best letters I ever received.'

'What was Robert Taylor like as your co-star?'

'Well, I didn't really know him.'

'I read somewhere that he dropped you on the floor when you were reshooting the death scene.'

'Well, he didn't. He was a very well brought up young man, a bit shy perhaps. He did everything to make me feel better. I was often actually rather ill during filming. He used to have a gramophone with him that he would play because he knew I liked music. It helped distract me. A film studio is pretty much like a factory, you know . . . and you are supposed to be soulful in the midst of all the din.

'Robert Taylor was from Nebraska. And he told me that his best friend during his youth in Nebraska had been a Swede. I have never liked sitting in the sun. I have a delicate skin and have to be careful not to get sunburnt. But Robert Taylor was the exact opposite. He worshipped the sun. And then he was forced to abstain from the outdoor life for the weeks we were filming since we both had to be equally pale.

'Robert Taylor was actually a kind and well-bred man. I really appreciated what he did when he visited Stockholm for the première of *Camille,* which was to send flowers to my mother, twelve gorgeous orchids.

'George Cukor was the director and put the film together in a very skilful way. I had great confidence in him. He taught me a lot even though he could suddenly become rather impatient.

'We had to make two different endings to the film—well, actually there were three. In one version I got to say more on my death-bed. In another version I had to be quieter and just slowly slip away. They plumped for the latter version and we were all in agreement on that point. It didn't really feel very natural talking that much when you've just about given up the ghost. . . .

'And Cukor also gave me direction as to how to hold my hands. He had seen how when his mother lay dying she folded her hands and just fell asleep . . .

'Robert Taylor didn't live to be all that old, you know. I never saw him again once filming was over. But I know he smoked too much, just like me, and he got lung cancer. He wasn't quite sixty when he died. I read that Ronald Reagan, who knew him, gave a very good speech at his funeral. This was when Reagan was Governor of California.'

We were sitting eating dinner at the Grill of the Pardenn Hotel. I had with me a number of film stills in an envelope, including some from *Camille*, which I took out to hear what Garbo thought of them. But although she was in a very good mood, she pushed the photos away and said, 'I don't want to see old film stills, but what you may do is take me to Normandy. It is in Normandy that they say Alphonsine became immortal when she died.'

The world really is a very small place: when my wife and I were wandering around the village where the Lady of the Camellias lived when she was a girl, we were finally directed to a very old and lovely house in the village of St Germain de Clairfeuille near Nonant, which was built on the very spot where the Lady of the Camellias had spent her childhood in such humble circumstances. The place is one of the most beautiful I have ever seen, although the local people say that there is blood in the ground: the German invasion during the Second World War reached this far.

We knocked on the door and introduced ourselves. A kind gentleman invited us in, a M. Jean-Claude Fleury.

'Yes, that's right: it was on this spot that the Lady of the Camellias lived as a child in a little shack . . . Are you from Sweden? It was a Swedish woman, after all—Greta Garbo—who made the Lady of the Camellias famous in our day.

'As it happens I'm very keen on Sweden. I used to work for Mo & Domsjö in France selling paper and I would travel up to

Ångermanland now and then to say hello. Would you like to join me for a calvados and we can drink to Sweden and to the Lady of the Camellias?'

I hardly ever saw Garbo as happy as on that evening. Even though we had mostly talked about death.

9

'I Ought To Make Another Film; I Won't Be A Good Match Otherwise'

Garbo was one of the many people who lost money in the stock-market crash in the USA in 1932. One of the reasons she went on working was in order to reach a state of financial security—the goal, or rather, the dream, of many people who have grown up with financial problems.

Garbo told Carl Johan Bernadotte that someone at MGM had recommended she buy shares in the First National Bank of Beverly Hills, which collapsed. She did not have all her assets in the bank—but a significant amount.

On 28 July 1934 Garbo wrote to her friend Hörke Wachtmeister that she had just started shooting *The Painted Veil* (adapted from a novel by Somerset Maugham): 'Rubbish—the film, I mean.'

In the letter Garbo dryly states:

I am still not rich enough . . . The only natural thing for me to do right now would be to disappear from films and get people to forget totally that I ever existed— I mean so that no one would look at me on the street . . .

. . . But I ought to make another film; I won't be a good match otherwise.

She goes on to express her homesickness once again:

We've got to find me a place, Hörke. Could you be a darling and have a look round and see if there isn't some wonderful old estate I could move into.

I've never had a home. I think that if I had one, I'd be calmer.

I understand that Garbo had phenomenally good hearing and that this could sometimes be a problem for her. In the same letter she complains about the birds outside her bungalow beginning to sing at four a.m. They made an ugly, penetrating noise, which meant she did not get enough sleep and would 'come stumbling on to the stage a few hours later'.

Garbo had a tendency to express herself rather dramatically both in speech and in writing.

Now and again film companies and others would get in touch with the Wachtmeister family and ask them to put proposals and offers to Garbo:

Dear Hörke.
Let me say thank you for the letter with the offer of engagement from London. There's no need for you to reply to that kind of thing, but if you are in touch personally with the His Majesty's Theatre people in London, you can just say that you don't know my plans and don't want to get involved in any negotiations.
God bless you,
The Clown.

A few weeks later, when the 'silly' film *The Painted Veil* had been finished, Garbo wrote once again:

I'm lying on a table in my so-called garden. I say so-called because it is extremely small and has nothing in common

with what a 'star' would call a gar-
den . . .

. . . My only joy is a tomato field below
the house I've rented. I go down there
doggedly when the cottage feels too
cramped. Sounds like a poem, doesn't it?

It may be hard for other people to be-
lieve, but my only diversions are my to-
mato field and a few scorched piles of
sand . . .

. . . Oh, it's such a pity that I'm not
home. I think about it and long for it
every moment. But prostitutes are never
very happy. I've already been back here
for more than two and a half years now
and have only made two films. It's that
awful contract I signed and I can do noth-
ing about it . . .

. . . I don't suppose you, Mrs Hörke,
have any idea that you have to pay half
of what you earn in taxes. I say that so
that you will understand why I have to
make a new film. And since I'm going to
remain unmarried, it's as well to be as
good a match as possible . . .

. . . But I am definitely coming back to
my homeland at the beginning of June.
Do you, dear Mrs Hörke, know of any
solitary country house that I can rent?

My brother is looking as best he can, but they are not easy to find. I wish I were related to Tistad and dreadfully popular and had never seen a film and had a decent fortune and could celebrate Christmas at Tistad.

The following extracts are from various letters:

Here's yet another piece of paper. It's Sunday and I am lying on a table that has been placed on the lawn. It's so hot you almost get boiled alive.

I have been thinking a bit enviously of that pier of yours where you're bound to be at this moment. I expect something happened to make you talk about me, since I spent an awful lot of time yesterday thinking about you all.

There's another thing I'd like to bother you with. I've been thinking about a place we once saw. I can't remember what it was called, but I think it belonged to Tessin and was called something like Åkerö . . .
. . . We went there one Sunday and there

were three people in the courtyard. We didn't speak to anyone. You have to go over a bridge or something like that to get there.

I wonder if maybe that place wasn't 'it'.

I wonder if you wouldn't mind asking, if it is financially viable, if it is for sale, whether you wouldn't mind telling my brother about it. He could go and have a look at it. In return I'll invite you to coffee—God willing.

Do write often—or none of you will get any coffee.

The Wachtmeister family found a temporary home for Garbo, Ånga House, a lovely place by the sea. The house was then owned by Olof Palme's mother, Elisabeth Palme. It was built in the functional style and had been exhibited at the Stockholm Exhibition in 1930. Garbo lived there for a couple of summer months in the thirties, at a convenient distance from Tistad Castle.

Her stay at Ånga House proved to be one of the most anonymous visits Garbo ever made to Sweden. But then the whole process of moving in was carried out very discreetly. Garbo arrived at Tistad Castle as usual with an impressive amount of luggage, suitcases and chests. Countess Hörke Wachtmeister got dressed up as a porter and Garbo concealed her identity with a pulled-down hat and a collar that could be folded up over half her face.

The staff at Tistad were, as ever, absolutely fascinated by the fact that Garbo once again kept special watch over a package she always brought with her—a set of bathroom scales from Hollywood. Self-control and will-power are what you need to be a beauty symbol for the whole world.

In a later (April 1937) letter from Hollywood Garbo wrote:

I am incredibly tired of being a 'star', tired of the films they offer me here, just tired in a word. But I am not satisfied with what I've got in the way of money, so I'll have to keep working for a while longer . . .

. . . My latest physician is a little hunchbacked man who I am dragging down into the abyss of pessimism. He sees me as an 'interesting case of depression.' He says he is a psychologist and wants to

help me in that way. He keeps me for an hour and a half every time.

We sit there fencing with words and keeping a watchful eye on one another. One day when I was very tired, I said, 'Everything is futile.'

'Yes, that's true,' he said.

But then he realized that was not the right way to treat a 'depression', so he gave me a piercing look and said one had to look at life with a sense of humour . . .

. . . My last hunt was at Tistad. But that time it was a fox that was shot. There are only lions here at MGM so I'm not interested.

Garbo wrote three letters to Hörke while she was working on *Camille* in 1936.

Gunnila Bernadotte says that her parents helped Garbo's brother Sven to buy the Hårby estate by Lake Sillen in the area round Gnesta in the county of Södermanland. The vendor was the wholesaler John Meuller and the price was 276,000 kronor. This included livestock comprising thirty cows, ten drays and chickens. There were about a thousand acres of land, including about one hundred and sixty acres of arable land. The property also comprised four

153

smallish lakes called Rinn, Mag, Bud, and Löf (which had crayfish).

Garbo wrote:

I am so pleased Sven found a house and I want to thank you from the bottom of my heart for all your help. It's as though a huge weight has been lifted from my chest. I really do want to express my thanks properly . . .

It is a bit difficult for me to make up my mind about the little house without having seen it

Hörke Wachtmeister had sent Garbo pictures of a smaller house that was for sale and was close by Tistad Castle.

If I were up to it and didn't have to go to bed for all these weeks, I'd have got on a boat and come home for a few weeks to see it . . .

. . . When your letter chose to arrive on my birthday I felt that a higher power wanted me to be happy. If I had been home I would have bought the house as a symbol of happiness . . .

. . . If I hadn't been so out of sorts Camille *would have been one of my most*

entertaining memories thanks to the director [George Gukor]. He is really extraordinarily nice. He looks so funny with his huge hips and his woman's breasts.

I'll soon be finished with the whole thing and blessed be the memory. There you are—that proves I'm not always ungrateful.

With a bit of help from the lord, I'd almost managed to forget to tell you that I am going to start the next film roughly seven weeks after we finish The Lady of the Camellias. *I've got no idea what will happen after that, but I will definitely come home . . .*

. . . Is Naima [Wifstrand] still in London?

You never tell me anything about what is happening to people at home. But then nothing does happen—as we always said in the film of Grand Hotel: 'People come and go, but nothing happens at the Grand Hotel.' . . .

. . . When I put the snaps away, I do it hoping against hope that the house will not have been sold by the time I come home.

Garbo had quite a few problems during

the filming of *Camille*. In another letter to Hörke she wrote:

I am so busy. I've got no time for any-thing other than Camille *and my health. I have never worked under conditions like these before. I sometimes start crying from tiredness. I leave home at about 8 a.m. and don't get home before 8 p.m. I've been feeling out of sorts the whole of last month and still had to work. I have been getting treatment after my hours at the studio but don't know if it helped or made it worse. At the moment I'm lying in bed—as usual when the moon's up . . .*
. . . Do write and tell me if you've still got the calf-box down at Larsson's. My writing's a bit confused but what can you expect from a lady of the camellias.

I wear the grey boy's cap I got from Hörke every day to the studio and almost feel as though I were home. God knows what I would have done without it . . .

Thanks so much for the details about Åkerö [Tessin's castle] but I don't really want such a big place myself . . .
. . . Who would have believed that it would be so difficult to find a property. The nicest one I remember was the one

156

THE TWENTY-THREE-YEAR-OLD GARBO,
WHOSE FAVORITE FORM OF CLOTHING
WAS TROUSERS, SEEN IN
THE SINGLE STANDARD
SHOWING HER LEGS FOR ONCE.

· · · · · ·

GARBO IN THE SILENT VERSION OF
ANNA KARENINA, KNOWN IN ENGLISH AS
LOVE, WHICH WAS PREMIERED ON
29 NOVEMBER 1927. MGM RETITLED THE FILM **LOVE**
SO THAT THE PUBLICITY MATERIAL COULD READ
"GRETA GARBO AND JOHN GILBERT IN **L O V E**."
· · · · · · · · ·

GARBO WITH COUNT NILS,
BOTH ARE HOLDING
PUPPIES.

· · · ·

GARBO—THE PERFECT BEAUTY—
IN THE SILENT FILM
THE MYSTERIOUS LADY,
PREMIERED IN AUGUST 1928.
VICTOR SJÖSTRÖM WAS THE DIRECTOR AND
GARBO PLAYED A RUSSIAN SPY.

· · · · · ·

GARBO WAS PARTIALLY RECONCILED TO
THIS PUBLICITY STILL FROM HER FIRST YEAR
IN HOLLYWOOD.
THE MAN IS JANNES ANDERSSON FROM MORA IN
DALECARLIA, WHO WAS A MASSEUR
AT THE TIME AT MGM.
'IT WAS A GOOD THING TO KNOW HIM,
ESPECIALLY IF YOU'D FALLEN OFF
YOUR HORSE AND HURT YOURSELF, WHICH
DID HAPPEN,' SAID GARBO.

. . . . . .

GARBO WAS KIND TO THE NEW YORK PRESS
ON HER RETURN TO THE USA FROM SWEDEN
ON THE *KUNGSHOLM* ON 7 OCTOBER 1938.
THAT WAS THE YEAR SHE HAD BEEN
TO ITALY AND SWEDEN WITH LEOPOLD
STOKOWSKI. GARBO WAS CHEERFUL
BUT HAD NOTHING TO TELL THEM.
HER GREYISH-BLUE WOOLLEN TIGHTS,
HOWEVER, DREW A GREAT DEAL
OF PUBLIC ATTENTION.

· · · · · ·

GEORGE CUKOR TAKES GARBO THROUGH A SCENE
IN **TWO-FACED WOMAN**, GARBO'S LAST
FILM, MADE IN 1941.

· · · · · · · ·

THIS WAS ONE OF GARBO'S FAVORITE PICTURES FROM
CONQUEST. THIS WAS THE PICTURE
SHE GAVE TO MARIA SANDLER, THE WIFE
OF RICHARD SANDLER, THE FOREIGN
MINISTER, WHOM SHE MET ON A SEA
VOYAGE TO NEW YORK IN 1937.

. . . .

GARBO AS THE SPY, MATA HARI (1931).
HER FIFTEENTH FILM FOR MGM,
MATA HARI BEAT ALL
GARBO'S PREVIOUS ATTENDANCE RECORDS.
GARBO WORE THIS SLICKED-BACK HAIRSTYLE
IN THE FINAL SCENES OF THE FILM, AS SHE WAS
BEING TAKEN OFF TO HER EXECUTION.

. . . .

A TYPICAL PICTURE OF GARBO FROM HER
LATER YEARS. PHOTOGRAPHED WHILE
OUT ON A WALK BEFORE SHE MANAGED TO HIDE
BEHIND HER UMBRELLA.

· · · · · ·

*we saw with Mercedes [d'Acosta], but
they didn't want to sell. Do you remember the one with the stone wall and all
the rest of it?*

The house on the Hårby estate was ready
to move into by 1 January 1937. It was an
idyllic place and archetypically Swedish.
The intention was to rent out the farming
to other farmers. The estate comprised extensive grounds and bordered on a large
forested headland stretching out into Lake
Sillen.

In the neighbourhood it was said that
Garbo had forbidden hunting on her property. This would have meant failure for the
hunters on the elk hunt: all the elks in the
area were concentrated on that tongue of
land—they were safe there.

Of course the whole thing was an exaggeration, but I told Garbo the story all the
same and she laughed out loud: 'I didn't
even know there were elks in those woods,
and I never forbade anyone to hunt on our
grounds. It sounds like what you might expect an elk hunter who comes home empty-
handed to say by way of explanation'

That headland (with its alleged elks)
stretching into the lake was called Tors-

näset and had been bought separately by Garbo.

Inga Lagerström, one of the first three photographic models in Sweden, explained that her parents lived by Lake Sillen and owned the headland with all its forests: 'Greta Garbo and her brother came suddenly one day to visit us. My sister was so astonished that she dropped a whisk and a sauce-bowl on the floor. Garbo smiled. It turned out that Garbo had been troubled by curious people looking at her from our headland and she wondered whether she could buy it. It was quite a large forested area that my parents sold to Garbo for thirteen thousand kronor. The headland today is worth closer to one million.'

Close to the lake is an impressive rock formation that is now called the Garbo Rock. Nature has carved a bench into the granite and that is where Garbo used to sit and relax on her own.

The farming land attached to Hårby Manor was to provide a whole new experience for Sven Gustafsson and his family, who came from Stockholm. He, too, got on well with the family at Tistad and Garbo was to write:

I've just had a short letter from my brother, who, by the way, writes as rarely as I do. So an awful lot of things can happen before I get to know about them.

He asked me a while ago if I thought that 'Yorkshire' (your husband) would let him have a look at the farming at Tistad so that he could learn a bit about running a farm. I said he could ask if it was all right and that he should make sure to hire the cottage that Hörke and I were offered by the Undsets [Garbo's nickname for the family of Sigrid Böklin]. *An old one to the left of the Undsets' own 'manor'.*

In December 1936 Garbo wrote:

Hello and Happy Christmas!
As always at this time of year image after image keeps rolling up in my imagination about what it's like where you all are. I can see masses of snow, but maybe that's wrong. And as always I want to go sleigh-riding.

I'll soon have to be off in the car. Camille never ends. We have to shoot retake after retake and are going to do some more in a couple of days. It's not ex-

159

actly a masterpiece either. She'll be arriving in Stockholm sometime towards the end of 1937 . . .

. . . Maybe you've simply forgotten me, all of you. Maybe you're finding Mrs Simpson so interesting that you've no time for anything else. Dear Mrs Simpson, now her quiet days are over. She'll be pursued now wherever she goes. Hope the camera-hunters will scare her so much that she'll leave my king in peace . . .

. . . It's December, soon it will be Christmas. I was brought up on Swedish food, schnapps as well, and here I sit waiting for an awful cold salad and nothing piquant in the way of a dressing to liven it up with . . .

. . . Nothing new has happened apart from Mercedes wanting me to ring. But I am going to have a think about the matter first. Poor Mercedes—she has got an extraordinary ability to make people nervous. Even people who are not quite as unkind as me.

. . . But it is Christmas and I would like to wish you all a very specially happy Christmas, since I can't be with you. When you go off to drink the first mulled wine of the season, don't forget that I

want you to drink my health, i.e. I'm asking you now.

Don't forget and don't drink to Mrs Simpson instead— because even if I'm not watching you, the heavens are.

Only one God. He created everything out of one spirit—we are all one. And God is love. Don't laugh (I'll explain when we see each other).

Happy Christmas to everyone at Tistad.

I forgot to say that I would desperately love to be there . . .

At the beginning of 1937 Garbo wrote a letter in which the influence of Mercedes d'Acosta and her Indian guru can be discerned:

I would like to travel to India and become wise. Finished Camille in December and am going to start my new film at any moment . . .

. . . I am doing various things in order to be 'well', but I am a bit down now and then. If I went to India maybe I would get some idea about how to master one's own body.

Say hello to Lasse [Gunnila Wacht-

161

meis*ter*-Bernadotte was called Lasse by her brothers and by Garbo] *and tell her that she made me so happy when she wrote to me.*

She looks like a grown-up lady. Can't you stop her from growing up too quickly? . . .

. . . Wolmar Boström [Sweden's ambassador to Washington] *informed me by letter about my being honoured.* [Garbo received the Order of Arts and Letters at Christmas 1936.]

I sent the following reply:

'Thank you for your telegram. May I ask the ambassador to pass on my most profound gratitude to His Majesty the King.'

I went on to wish him, the ambassador, Happy New Year. If this is insufficient, please could you write and tell me so.

I haven't received the 'medal' yet.

In the summer of 1937 Garbo wrote that it was incredibly warm but that nothing smelt of summer. She longed for forests and lakes and coolness.

Don't forget if you see some wonderful

*place to think of me and then we'll
buy it.*

. . . And then she starts longing for Värm-
land, but has instead to try on clothes:

*. . . and the ugliest hairstyles and hats
(1847). But I expect I'll be able to put together a bastard version of the styles, although I really do want to do it all
correctly. Anyway they are all convinced
I have finished with films after* Camille.
*So if you only care about me because of
'my glory in film' think it over.*

*I have just spent the last week in bed
with my usual trouble. God help the soldier—have been to see Bieler, who looked
very sulky, perhaps because I am not
looking after myself like I should. I believe in him like I do Buddha . . .* [Dr.
Harold Bieler of Pasadena was Garbo's doctor for many years. Among
the things he prescribed for her was
eating vegetables.]
*. . . God , how I long for my summer
home.*

*Say hello to Lasse and everyone at
Tistad including Herr Larsson . . .*

Hörke and her husband were really given a lot of insights into a large part of Garbo's life, her dreams and plans. In the spring of 1938 Garbo met the world-famous conductor of the Philadelphia Orchestra, Leopold Stokowski, and agreed to travel to Europe with him.

In a letter from Ravello, in southern Italy, of 17 March 1938 Garbo asked Hörke to look at a little flat on Djurgärden in Stockholm that her brother, Sven, had rented for her:

If it isn't very nice, maybe it can be rented out.

Garbo, now thirty-two, was in Italy with Stokowski, who was fifty-six. They were planning to visit Sweden:

As for me, I am really very sad . . .

One thing is clear, I have to stop making films. I cannot go on this way. I haven't seen a thing and I have been away far too long.

The only way out of this current prison I'm in is to meet the press and with God's help I shall do so tomorrow. We'll have to see how it goes. You cannot have anything for yourself in this strange world of ours people have done so much to destroy . . .

. . . There's one more thing. If you should hear about a plot of land I could have a cottage built on, please save it for me. I have to have somewhere of my own as soon as possible. I am ready now to withdraw completely, but I must have something already built . . .

. . . I am sorry I didn't stay at home in the USA, but I am so polite to friends and acquaintances once I've got to know them. And when they have got plans like going to Italy, I can't say no.

The story of Garbo's and Stokowski's European journey was taken up by the world's press every day.

On 25 April 1938 Garbo wrote from Paris:

Dear Mrs Hörke,
Not that I know whether you are at home or in China, but I was wondering whether you would be kind enough to have me and another person to lunch when we 'travel through Sweden.'

What I would like most is if you were to meet me in southern Sweden, but I re-

165

ally can't ask that of you so we'll leave it be. If I can send you a wire later on maybe you could come and pick me up. We're driving, but we could arrange another empty seat in the car. If I wire you the name and date of the meeting place, you'll know it is from me and then you can do as you like. With 'God's help' it'll be around the beginning of May or maybe a little bit later.

I have no idea whether there is anything in the papers. I hope it's quiet. Don't know anything either about what's happening in the world. Hope that's peaceful, too. I don't think I want to go abroad anymore, possibly if we could travel together to Norway but we'll 'talk that over' (Swedish-Americanism) when we meet.

Hope you are all well and that you haven't forgotten me totally.

Dear Mrs Hörke, when I come to Tistad please can I have lots of lettuce if you've got any of course and vegetables. I long for my vegetables and my special diet again. I know you don't want to hear that but that is how it is.

So I'll wire you if possible and see if you can come to meet me.

Other engagements prevented Hörke from meeting Garbo and Stokowski when they arrived. According to plan they had driven across Europe and arrived in southern Sweden on the ferry from Sassnitz on 5 May at six-thirty a.m. Stokowski, who had registered as a 'person of independent means', had hired a grey-green Lincoln Zephyr in Italy and was doing the driving. Garbo was the navigator.

Despite their customary security measures—pulled-down hats and drawn-up collars—soon everyone knew just which celebrities were on their way. Their first stop was at Lundholm's stationer's in Hammenhög, where Stokowski wanted to telephone Sven Gustafsson at Hårby Manor outside Gnesta. No one in the shop understood English and Garbo was forced to intervene:

'Is that Sven? Yes, we're arriving early tomorrow morning but not before nine o'clock, otherwise it will be a strain on mother.'

Rumour had it that the entourage would drive to Nyköping via Kalmar. A German Opel carrying two elderly, innocent Germans was stopped in Blekinge by Garbo fans.

Kristianstad was astir, so was Jönköping. But they actually drove a quite different way: Sölvesborg—Asarum—Tingsryd—Lessebo—Nottebäck to Vimmerby. That is where the navigatrix got confused and lost their way.

At midnight Stokowski decided to stop and ask the way to Nyköping, since they were heading for the second time for Valdemarsvik. There was a light on in a house in Söderköping— Stokowski braked to a halt. It turned out to be the editorial offices of the newspaper *Södeiköping-Posten*. The editor, Arthur Vindevåg, was sitting writing an article about American cinema-owners having started a boycott of those films featuring stars in Hollywood who were asking for too much money, including Greta Garbo. Yet he failed to recognize the stranger with the saintly white crest of hair who was suddenly standing in the doorway and asking: 'Niköping?'

Vindeväg thought the man said 'Linköping' and tried to sort the matter Out by asking: 'Do you speak English? *Sprechen Sie Deutsch?*'

But by the time he got to the door

Vindeväg had seen the woman in the car and although somewhat taken aback was able to point out the way to Nyköping.

Dagens Nyheter [the leading Swedish daily] had a lengthy feature on the drive through Sweden of the celebrity couple. This ended with a piece of news from the newspaper's New York correspondent, who reported that Garbo and Stokowski—according to inside information from Hollywood—were already married.

The next day *Dagens Nyheter's* front page led with a three-column headline that denied this: NO, GARBO IS NOT MARRIED!

Dagens Nyheter was nevertheless accorded an exclusive interview with the celebrated Stokowski. There were two conditions: the interview had to take place outdoors (no journalist was allowed into Hårby) and no personal questions were to be asked.

It started to pour with rain as *Dagens Nyheter's* star reporter Torsten Flodén (whose pseudonym was 'Cyrano') arrived at Hårby. Stokowski turned up swathed in waterproof clothing. He was wearing a bright-blue blazer with the red ribbon of the Legion of Honour shimmering at his buttonhole. Flodén managed to catch a glimpse inside Stokowski's car, where a map of Sweden lay spread out, with several arrows inked in, in various directions around Vimmerby.

Flodén's first question was: 'Which actress do you admire most?'

'That is a personal question and I won't answer it.'

After that their conversation turned to Stokowski's appreciation of Swedish folk music, the fact that he was negotiating with Walt Disney about a film, that he believed music to be an international force for peace, that he liked children and that he preferred working at night.

The interview took place in the course of a long walk along rain-soaked village paths. A few photographers taking snaps from the bushes were forced to surrender their films, which Stokowski trampled to bits.

Flodén, who had been tricked out of seeing Garbo and had got wet through in the pouring rain, ended his report by giving Hårby's steward—Sven Gustafsson—a ticking-off: 'When you have got such distinguished guests, the house flag really should be raised.'

On a couple of occasions Garbo and

Stokowski also stayed at Tistad Castle. In addition there were several events in Stockholm, including two meals on Djurgården: one at the old Bellmansro and one at Lower Manilla, the Bonniers' family home.

Åke Bonnier has written about his first meeting with Garbo in a private memoir:

Love Story
One summer day in 1938 I was rung up by a good friend Lennart Reuterskiöld, who owns the music publisher's Reuter and Reuter.

'I suspect you know that Garbo and Stokowski are in Stockholm and since I have a little business to do with Stokowski, I thought I would invite them to lunch. Would you like to join us to make up the four?'

Of course, I said yes and we had a very pleasant lunch at Bellmansro. We were seated in something that was, I think, called the 'Galley', below the main dining-room, so that Garbo could avoid being watched, which she found intimidating.

'It is so lovely at Lower Manilla where my parents live. Why don't you come out and dine there one evening?'

'We'd love to,' Garbo replied, 'but we're off on Saturday.'

'Well then, Friday, perhaps?'

'That would be lovely, thank you.'

Then I drove out to lower Manilla and only saw my mother, Lisen Bonnier, at first.

'Eva and I will be coming to dinner on Friday,' I said, if that is all right?'

'Of course, you are both very welcome . . .

'And we will have two Americans with us . . .

'And who are they?'

'Leopold Stokowski and Greta Garbo.'

'I am not so sure about that, you know, I don't think your father would like that. You'll have to ask him. He's lying down having a rest at the moment.' [Åke Bonnier's father was the publisher Karl-Otto Bonnier.]

I waited till he woke up and then went in to him and said:

'Father, Eva and I are coming to dinner on Friday.'

'That is nice,' he replied.

'And we will have two guests with us . . .'

'Well, of course, they're welcome. And who might they be?'

Leopold Stokowski and Greta Garbo.'

'Greta Garbo, I don't think I would like

that, you know, I never go and see films and I am not interested in film stars. Take them out to the Grand Hotel or have them at your home.'

'But, Father, you know that in summer the furniture at our place is all under covers, and they are having to stay at a hotel already, so that's no fun. And it is just so lovely out here at the moment.'

My father was rather upset and did not want to discuss the matter, but in the end he gave in to my persistent entreaties:

'Well, if you're going to force me, I'll have to put up with it.'

It was a fabulously beautfull day at the beginning of August. On days like that the table would be laid out on the terrace. Garbo arrived in long white trousers, which were considered rather startling in those days. My father was obliged to have Garbo sit next to him. Garbo turned out to be in a very lively and pleasant and talkative mood. Afier dinner she said to my father: 'Now you must show me the garden.'

And she took him under the arm and they took a tour round the garden and had a look at the greenhouse.

They were gone a good while and then we

sat in the library and chatted, before Eva and I drove our guests home.

It got quite late and it was gone one in the morning when we got home. The telephone suddenly started to ring and I thought: who could it possibly be ringing at this time of night?

It was my father, who said in that aged, trembling voice of his (he was over eighty-two years old): 'Thank you, dear Åke, for forcing me to have Greta Garbo to dinner, you see, I have fallen so dreadfully in love with her.'

When we talked about her memories of Sweden with Garbo in Klosters, she herself brought up the dinner at Lower Manilla: 'I was invited, you know, to a very posh dinner at your former employer's, Mr Broman, I with the Bonnier family. It was very embarrassing as I was all dressed in white, with long white trousers . . . It was considered dreadfully unsuitable for a lady to appear in long trousers at an event of that kind in the thirties.'

Their hosts at Tistad felt the couple were very attached to one another, but they also knew that Garbo found it difficult to make up her mind. In May of the following year, she wrote from Hollywood:

174

Dear Lady,

. . . My studio is starting to collapse be-cause everything is in chaos. I should have started work in November but noth-ing gets finished.

It is miserable having to live your life and spend your time in this way, but I have been putting out my plants instead.

I have no idea what will happen to me but there's a little angel somewhere who is changing my life—I do not know into what.

I think so often about Tistad.

And then there is a little passage about Stokowski ('my friend'):

My friend will be coming to Sweden soon. Although by the time you get this note at Tistad he may already have been there. I haven't seen him for a long time. He has been staying in New York the last few months. Perhaps you'll go and hear him—in that case do let me know what it was like. I've never 'seen' him con-duct . . .

. . . How is Yorkie's mother? I think about her sometimes and wonder whether she looked up that doctor in Gothenburg I told her about. As for me personally, I

take pills as well, though under pro-
test . . .

. . . I have been a bit down the last few
days due to nerves perhaps or God knows
what. But it is getting better and better.

Us poor moderns (though perhaps it
has always been like this) we have to live
with so much anxiety inside ourselves but
maybe in a couple of million years things
will be as they should be . . .

. . . I really would love to go swimming
with you again, even when there's a thunderstorm. I have so many wondel memories of Tistad . . .

Dear Hörke, do write and tell me
about everything, about the trees and the
water and the animals and Larsson and
what you've got in the cellars and in the
apple-shed.

10

I Was Garbo's Psychologist

Unlike in Sweden, people in America have always been candid about their relationships with doctors. It has always been the done thing to seek medical help for nervous problems or sleeplessness. It was to be a Swedish psychologist, Dr Eric Drimmer, who would for a six-month period provide help of this kind for Greta Garbo.

Drimmer, who was born in Järvsjö, worked in the USA for ten years from 1939 to 1945, spending most of this period in Hollywood. For a short while he was married to Eva Gabor, the sister of Zsa-Zsa. Drimmer was hired by MGM, and his patients included Clark Gable and Robert Taylor. He had started as a physiotherapist: in 1928 he graduated from the Institute of Physical Culture in Gothenburg. He continued his studies in Germany and later in England and the USA.

Drimmer trained in what was known as

morphology, which was a study of the human body aimed at creating harmony in the individual. In both his person and character he resembled the stereotype of the powerful, blond Viking. He finished his studies at Emerson College in the USA, where he gained his doctorate.

Garbo got in touch with Drimmer and was his patient for six months in 1939-40. She wanted help for her nerves ('relief from nervous tension' was what was noted in the casebook).

'Garbo is a wonderful person,' said Dr Drimmer. 'She is reserved and stand-offish, but once she has opened up you feel she is talking straight from the heart. This makes a very strong impression on you. I saw her as a restless person, always looking for and never finding a foothold in life.'

After his brief marriage to Eva Gabor, Drimmer met in the USA a girl from Östersund, Maj-Britt Thorsell, known as 'Pomme'. They got married, moved back to Sweden and started a family.

Apart from an interruption of a few years when Drimmer, on the recommendation of Prince Wilhelm, started a practice in Monte Carlo, he went on working in Stockholm until his death in 1967. For most of her life, Mrs Drimmer's work was arranging art exhibitions in Europe and the USA.

Dr and Mrs Drimmer kept in touch with Garbo long after she ceased to be a patient and she saw the family whenever she visited Stockholm.

'The last time was in 1962,' Mrs Drimmer said. 'Garbo was out walking on Djurgården with Einar Nerman. Suddenly she felt like freshly baked waffles and jam. "The Drimmers can fix that", Einar said. So they came here and having a guest as pleased as Garbo made being the hostess very gratifying. She ate her waffles with all the delight of a child.'

It is worth mentioning that the two actors who made the strongest impression on Drimmer in Hollywood apart from Garbo were Charlie Chaplin and Mickey Rooney: 'Just think of it, a little fellow like Mickey Rooney, only five feet tall and with a snub nose who manages to make himself the centre of every stage, how ever many other people are lined up with him. Talk about personality.'

In 1959, under his own name, Eric Drimmer published an article about Garbo for the, Swedish Magazine *Året Runt*. If anyone could, he was the one to refute some of the speculation about Garbo and he was to state: 'I say this with absolute conviction: Greta Garbo herself never had anything to do with creating the myth of her solitude. It was created by other people.'

Drimmer's aim was to help Garbo—as with any other patient—to restore harmony between body and mind. He discovered that her passion for solitude had reached such an extent that her friends risked never seeing her again if they revealed the slightest thing about her private life.

'As I became familiar with her problems, I grew increasingly convinced that Greta Garbo suffered from a shyness *vis-à-vis* the world around her that bordered on the pathological. During our many long conversations, I also came to realize that the first step towards a change for the better in her health had to come from within herself. She had to reveal openly her fear, not hide behind it or call it something else.

'There is no doubt that it was the worldwide publicity attached to the Garbo name that was the source of her anxiety. That is why I tried very seriously to persuade her to break through her feelings of terror using the same means, i.e. by discussing her problem openly and in public. It would only be then, I said, that she would be able to live like a normal person.

'People who describe Garbo's shyness as a pose do not have the faintest idea what they are talking about. I can assure you that the different ways she would react to various situations were as much a mystery to her as to anyone else. It was to find an explanation for all that she could not understand in her own personality that she consulted me.

'If a normal human being is suddenly faced with a dangerous wild animal, that person will experience intense fear. That is exactly what Garbo felt when faced with a crowd of people. A few strangers pushing forward to get autographs, and even her colleagues, on occasion, could fill her with terror. Her sole impulse was to turn and flee.'

Drimmer's talks with Garbo helped to make the picture clearer:

'The more I came to know about her past and heard her story, the more convinced I became that Garbo was a normal, ambitious and cheerful girl when she left Sweden. Hollywood was solely responsible for her inhibitions. No matter how paradoxical it may sound, her life took a wrong direction just at the point at which her fame and wealth were created.

'In the beginning there was no more mystery surrounding Greta Garbo than around any other young girl who suddenly appeared in Hollywood and was thrust into the limelight. She was not used to the hard pace and the "toughness" of that huge country. She was confused by the inquisitiveness of the press and when they misunderstood and ridiculed her limited English vocabulary she was happy to be allowed to escape interviews and public appearances. But there was one thing that she soon discovered: it is always difficult to live up to your public image. The same thing applies whether you are an actress or a politician.

'The mysterious Garbo was not allowed to appear in public. If she did, she would not have been mysterious, a role she was now stuck with. She was famous, richer than she could ever have dreamed and she longed for adventure. But she was a prisoner of the myth that surrounded her. Slowly the walls around her closed in. The legend of her, mysteriousness that started as a form of protection became a complex, an *idée fixe*.

'When Garbo was not working, her life was based on a strict routine. She got up at six o'clock and spent ten minutes doing yoga and breathing exercises. After a breakfast consisting of a single glass of fruit juice, her chauffeur drove her to the beach, which at that time of the morning was totally deserted. She would go swimming and go for a walk that could stretch for many miles along the beach. When she got hungry, she would return to the car. On the back seat there was always a large wooden bowl filled with a salad of raw vegetables, mixed with a dressing of olive oil, lemon and salt as well as a packet of Swedish crispbread.

'Whenever Garbo went for a long drive she would take the bowl of salad with her in the car instead of stopping at a restaurant to eat lunch. It was only the privileged few who were allowed to share these salad meals. Einar Nerman and his wife belonged to this select company.

'Garbo usually went to bed very early. She would often go to bed at seven in the evening, just as things were stirring in Hollywood. She loved reading in bed and she would often read heavyweight stuff that was pretty demanding. She made a thorough study of philosophy. There were many occasions when she and I would talk about Indian philosophy and yoga and she confided in me that she had a thirst to get to know more about the secrets of life that was never satisfied. It was this that drove her to attend a series of lectures that were given by a swami—an Indian philosopher—in a temple high up in the Verdugo hills in California.

'As soon as she left Hollywood, Garbo would blossom, she would relax and become more open. I know that she planned to spend most of her time in Sweden once she had got a contract that allowed her to pick and choose from the films offered her. But war intervened. Instead she brought her mother and brother and sister-in-law over to the the USA. She installed them in a house in the Montecino hills above Santa Barbara and made frequent visits there to spend time together with them.

'Taking his mother with them, Sven Gustafsson and his family moved fairly soon afterwards to New Mexico for health reasons. The climate there was drier and made breathing easier.

'Garbo's physical fitness was exceptionally good and of course it was not harmed by her both resting and taking a lot of exercise. She had enormous vitality and although like most stars she had to keep her weight down she always used to eat whatever she liked.

'Laughing, a good friend told me one day that he had been eating lunch at Perrino's, an elegant restaurant on Wilshire Boulevard. He had noticed a girl sitting alone at a table opposite him. Instead of using her fork she ate with a dessert spoon and almost shovelled her food down, which consisted of a large helping of spaghetti, meatballs and masses of vegetables.

'It was Greta Garbo and it was obvious she was making no attempt to protect her anonymity. For dessert she ate two enormous portions of strawberry ice-cream.

'The news that Garbo had been seen eating in a restaurant gratified me, not so much because of her hearty appetite but because it seemed to indicate that she was beginning to get over her fear of being seen in the open in Hollywood. But perhaps the myth of her solitude was too firmly entrenched. Or perhaps she lacked the strength to fight her way out of it.'

11

'I Would Have Liked To Be A Countess'

Greta Garbo liked to talk about death. She was not afraid of dying. She loved life to the very end and wanted to go on living even when it had to be on a very low flame.

I got the chance to talk to Garbo about death as late as July 1988. We were sitting in the bar of the Hotel Pardenn. I was simply being polite when I asked her how she was (we had not spoken to one another for more than a couple of months) but she replied by giving me a very sober and matter-of-fact report: 'I am not very well. I regret coming to Switzerland. I should have stayed in New York, but I can't bear the heat in summer and I can't stand air-conditioning.

'We won't be able to go out in your car, Mr Broman, which I was so looking forward to. I am not up to it. I can only walk a few steps. I spend most of the time lying down in my room. I can't eat anything. I am in a daze. The life around me no longer seems real. It feels like I'm dying bit by bit.'

Despite this gloomy news about her health Garbo leant towards me and said in a low voice, 'Do make sure that she makes a proper drink.'

'She' was the cordial and attentive female bartender, Nina Piccino, a Yugoslav married to an Italian, who divided her life between Italy and Switzerland.

'I walk round the hotel for quarter of an hour with Mrs Friedlander, that's all I can manage.

'People learn to accept death. If you die in good health, then you have not been trained nor made ready for death, said an old philosopher.'

When I paid her a compliment and told her that she looked fine, she rejected it.

'Not so. It is just the bad lighting they have in every bar to sell more alcohol. I'll just nibble on a few nuts, but I won't have any more to drink. I have had my ration for the day. I often think about death. I really wish I could believe, but I can't. For me it's over when it ends. Maybe I am too prosaic.

'And yet I do feel that life has been good in my old age. Long ago I knew, a doctor who was very funny. He always said: "Be happy that you are in the second half of your life. Youth is largely wasted on the young!" '

Then Garbo started quite spontaneously to recite a poem by Harriet Löwenhjelm:

I am tired to death,
rather tired,
very tired,
sick and tired and sad.

The way I wandered was a long one,
I met no little friend.
I am tired,
rather tired,
sick and tired and sad.

The picture I am drawing of Garbo may seem a bit jumpy and disconnected, but Garbo had a very individual way of talking and telling stories that usually included some pretty major jumps—often between humour and seriousness. She was unpredictable and never boring.

I told her about my meeting a Swedish woman doctor, Christina Hjort, whose mother had won a film competition at the beginning of the thirties entitled 'Do you look like Greta Garbo?' MGM had got several countries to set up competitions of this kind.

'Maybe you have already read or even heard that Sophia Loren's mother in Naples won a similar competition in Italy. Sophia writes about it with pride in her memoirs,' Garbo said.

'Good heavens, what a nuisance I've caused. I once got a letter from a girl in a hilltop village in Italy, who wanted me to help her get into films. "Everyone in the village says I look like you," she wrote. She had dark, or rather, black hair that was plaited and she went on to say in her letter: "I can also yodel and speak backwards . . ." It's fun meeting people who aren't affected and pretentious.

'I'll never forget a lovely old lady I met in Dalecarlia. Hörke Wachtmeister and I drove one summer over to Mora, where I wanted to visit a man from Dalecarlia who had worked at MGM as a masseur for many years. He used to give me massage, as well. His name was Jannes Andersson. When we arrived at his home, he was out fishing and there was only his elderly mother at home.

I introduced myself and then she said: "Oh, that's what you look like, is it?"'

Garbo was a good listener. And she would not hesitate to ask if there was something she did not understand.

'I think that the whole of creation is so vast and so difficult to explain. I would like to believe in a life after death, but the different religions have each got their own different solution. In America people go to church a lot, but I don't know if they're any the more religious for all that.

'I know that there are many people who are convinced of life after death, but I haven't been given the capacity for belief This is the kind of thing I spend my time brooding about . . .

'What frightens me are the large number of dreadful preachers who appear on American television. There is one I do like though, but I can't remember his name.'

When we visited Klosters we used to arrange to have our newspapers forwarded. I used to pass our copies on to Garbo, who was keen to read a Swedish newspaper whenever she got the chance. The oddest things would grab her attention: 'Why is mince so dear in Sweden?'

One day *Dagens Nyheter* had devoted

nearly a whole page to the local government offices in Kramfors, where they had decided to ban smoking on the premises—or that is how Garbo had interpreted the article. She knew I came from Kramfors and I had been touting the idea of touring round Norrland (the northernmost province of Sweden) by car.

'Do you really still want me to go to Kramfors, Mr Broman? You can't even smoke there when you're on your own in a room.'

There went my chance to show Garbo the bridge at Sandö.

'I think that every created being has both a task to do and a right to exist,' she said, returning to her theme. 'I was reading in a newspaper about the problems to do with the destruction of the environment in East Germany. Nearly all the ladybirds had died as a consequence of chemical spraying of some kind. This had a bad effect on the rest of the animal kingdom. They were forced to import ladybirds to restore the balance.'

We got the impression that what Garbo wanted was help in finding proof of 'eternity', of a form of life after death. We were able to joke about it, too. A bit too heartily I tried to point out that there ought—or had—to be a heaven or some kind of life after death. But, I said, an old journalist like myself would, of course, have to be grateful even for standing-room only in heaven.

'No, I'm sure you'll get a seat of your own,' Garbo said generously.

'But most of the stuff in the papers is wrong. They once wrote that I had a car, the kind called a Duesenberg, specially fitted with a dressing-table. I have never had a Duesenberg.

'But Howard Hughes was quite fantastic. He managed to sort the journalists out and still hide away from the world.

'I once had a doctor who said I had problems with my liver and that I shouldn't drink alcohol. I abstained for six months, but then I couldn't bear it any longer. I contacted the doctor—who neither drank nor smoked—and asked him if I couldn't interrupt the punishment. Then he said I could drink a little wine . . . But I have never liked wine particularly.'

Garbo used to send herself up: she used to refer to whisky as 'mother's milk', or she would say, 'I have been to the doctor today. He found it difficult to draw any blood.'

She showed us one of her hands, on

which she had two sticking-plasters: 'But there wasn't any blood. He had to prick me in the armpit . . . there isn't much left of us . . . On top of it all my feet hurt as well. Not even handmade shoes from Ferragamo in New York can help. My feet still hurt.'

This was in the summer of 1988. We were lucky to arrive in Klosters as Garbo was getting bored with solitude and wanted to talk. As elderly people often do, Garbo went straight to the point. On one occasion she leant her head back and said, 'I would have liked to be a countess.

'A countess?'

'Yes, I would have liked to live in the country, to be protected and sheltered. I like animals. I want to have peace around me. I have mostly wanted to be alone so that I can have peace and quiet. You can't get that in big cities. But I don't think you can live on your own just anywhere in the country, which is why I chose to live in a large city, where you can hide yourself away. I often used to be a guest at Tistad in Södermanland before the war. Those were the best days of my life. But I have been so unenterprising. There have been so many days when I've not got out of bed . . . I just couldn't. Before you arrived, I hadn't been down to the dining-room one single day for a whole month. I have had my meals up in my room. And I haven't been well.'

We were sitting on our own with Garbo in the bar. There was a small dance-floor next to the bar and I was bold enough to do some tap-dancing.

'Oh, can you tap-dance?' said a surprised and delighted Garbo.

'No, I can't. But I am willing to give it a try to honour the memory of the late Fred Astaire.'

'Yes, he is gone. He was unique . . .'

Garbo was more open about breaking off her sentences like this in our company. Of course, we were not always so serious, but Garbo never liked gossiping. She preferred to stay silent.

She asked me what she should do with her Swiss money when she returned to New York. Should she change it into dollars here or in New York?

I regretted that I was unable to answer her question, and then she said: 'I usually put the Swiss francs I have got left over in the bottom of a suitcase when I get home. They are supposed to stay there until I come over here again. You mustn't think

I've got any money in one of the Swiss banks.'

Was Garbo socially aware? Yes she was—anyway she noticed more than you might think: 'In Switzerland people only think about themselves. In the course of the years I've been coming here I've noticed that it is the foreigners who get the worst jobs. And when they're no longer needed, they get sent away. It's clean and tidy here but also expensive and boring.'

'Well, in Sweden today, many immigrants have the worst jobs, as well.'

'Every country does have its own problems. Still, America has accepted people from every corner of the globe, although they've been a bit bureaucratic about it sometimes. Hollywood in the old days was made up of people of every conceivable nationality.

'But the worst thing is not being at home anywhere. For a long time I spent my summers on the Riviera. But I was so lazy and unenterprising that I never learnt French. I used to feel left out . . . and let me tell you I've almost never felt left out. But I can pretend. I learnt by heart a piece from a play in French. And I have been known to recite it, which led people to believe that

I spoke French.'

Then, with a perfect French intonation, Garbo recited an impressive monologue in her beautiful voice.

'But if you're Greta Garbo, surely you're made welcome wherever you go. Most people have to make do without that kind of esteem . . .'

'Pah, being a movie-star—and this applies to all them—means being looked at from every possible direction. You are never left in peace. You're just fair game.'

'On the subject of being fair game, I read somewhere that tickets used to be sold for the observation points at the relevant stations when you went by train across America.'

'Yes, that was the first time I went home to Sweden and it didn't only affect me. I was told about all that before I got on the train in Los Angeles, so I used to stay sitting hidden behind my coat as soon as the train stopped at a station. The aim was to let nosy people get a look at me from balconies when the train came to a halt.

'But I didn't travel that much, so it was other people who were exposed to it more. Arriving in New York could be difficult, but I used to get off the train before it got to Central Station and take a taxi to the hotel.'

It was not often that Garbo chose to talk freely about what had happened in the past. But it seemed to me that this reflected her need to illustrate why she wanted to live far from large concentrations of people and their noise.

12

'Life Could Be So Wonderful— If We Only Knew What To Do With It'

The world saw the outbreak of the Second World War on 1 September 1939. Five weeks later, on 7 October, Garbo wrote:

Dear Hörke,
. . . I was just on the point of leaving for home when the war broke out. They are reluctant to cross the Atlantic just now, so I'll have to wait. The whole time I believed it would quieten down again, but now I have my doubts. Hope to God our little country isn't drawn into the misery . . .
. . . I do so hope I'll be able to get Café Haag at Tistad again soon . . .
. . . My film [Ninotchka] is finished and I'm afraid it doesn't amount to much. And then of course they're marrying me

off again at the moment. My film enters the market-place and they have to marry me off. But as usual nothing happens. I remain a 'maid'—

My dear, you will pray particularly hard every evening that the world will soon be nice and calm, won't you?

Is Yorkie's mother all right now? . . .

. . . It's so awful thinking about what might happen if war came. So we will pray.

Of course the best thing would be if everyone on earth was nice all the time, then nothing would be difficult or complicated.

Keep well, Hörke, and say hello to Tistad from me.

You cannot help but be struck by Garbo's constant pessimism about the film she was making or had recently finished. *Ninotchka* is in many people's eyes Garbo's best film and is considered today to be one of the all-time classics. But they were pretty inured to this at Tistad castle. They knew that Garbo lacked self-confidence and that this was linked to a kind of superstitious incantation: 'If I start by having too much faith in it, it will end up going to hell.'

My wife and I came in contact with another, rather more playful side to Garbo's way of looking at things. She believed in numerology. It was odd numbers that mattered: one, three, five and so on. My birth date was given approval. And Garbo's own on 18 September becomes nine plus nine (the ninth month) so she was pleased about that as well. You cannot really accuse Garbo of being superstitious. But she liked to toy with ideas of this kind.

The war made Garbo feel all the more lost in Hollywood and this was reflected in a letter from Beverly Hills dated 14 November 1939. She had heard that men of military age were being called up for military service in Sweden as well:

Dearest Hörke,
You never write so I've no idea what things are like at home. I don't know why but I have this strong feeling that it is impossible that there will be a real war.
I still don't know what I am going to do about filming. I find working more difficult than ever. I don't know why that's so, but I am so embarrassed when I'm in the studio.

How's the farming at the moment?
Have you got any men to do the work?
Or has everything gone wrong? But the
country has to have food so I can't under-
stand what the plan is if they take the
workers off . . .

. . . I haven't set foot outside the local
neighbourhood. I am almost always alone
and talk to myself I drive to the beach
and take walks and that's always marvel-
lous. But that's it.

You might like to walk there with me.
But you are so far away.

I would like to be in Sweden at this
time of year. And were you to appear be-
fore me as St Lucia, then I would think
everything was really all right . . .

. . . Now and again I see a portrait of
Gustaf [the King of Sweden] *and then*
I feel homesick. Don't forget to pray to
the Lord for peace.

In much of Europe the war had been
going on since 1 September 1939. It would
be slightly more than two years before the
USA would join the war.

Garbo wrote to Hörke on 15 March
1940:

Sweden really isn't safe. I do so long to go home, but the ocean is so unsafe now . . .

. . . The family are living here only a day's journey away. Peg [her brother Sven's wife] *is having a lot of trouble with her joints and my brother and Mum want to go home.*

I've seen the Nermans [Einar Nerman and his family] *a couple of times and they're finding things difficult as well . . .*

. . . You probably read in the papers that I've been at the Wenner-Grens'. Sadly he was away. I think they're homesick, too, but I don't know that for sure.

They certainly did feel bitter at Sweden. But I've no idea what happened so I can't judge. But I got the feeling that they longed to go back to our country . . .

. . . I don't know what I'm going to do with myself I've kept away from the studio. If peace comes, what I most want is to go home and not to make another film. I don't even want to think about it.

It is worth pointing out that Garbo wrote

that she wanted to quit Hollywood shortly after her success in *Ninotchka*, even before she had begun work on her last film, *Two-Faced Woman*.

She goes on to write:

Do write again soon if you want to and have got the time. You're the only one who can send me any word from Sweden . . .

. . . So don't forget me although I haven't been good and done my bit for Finland. I couldn't throw myself into it. I wouldn't have lasted.

The Wachtmeister family realized that it made more sense than ever to send Garbo Swedish newspapers, isolated as she was. They sent her various newspapers and *Filmjournalen* (Garbo liked to do its crossword.)

On 22 April 1940, Garbo wrote:

Darling Hörke,
Thank you for your letters and papers and articles. I am so pleased you send them . . .

. . . I read the papers for news, but not everything they print is true.

If only this nightmare were over. I can't work. I'm still lazy or looking for peace within. But I am going to pop in soon and say hello to the people at work. I haven't been there for five months.

Time passes quickly. I want to go home so much.

What will happen to people at home if something does happen, your sister's husband, for example? But it is simply thoughtless of me to ask . . .

Hörke, if everything is all right and you've got the time, could you be a darling and send me some Chropax earplugs. I can't get them here or in New York. I'd like six boxes, if that's possible, and I'll make a note in my little black book that I owe you masses of money.

Garbo would return over and over again to those Chropax ear-plugs. She had the hearing of a child of nature, she could hear everything. In the latter part of her life one of the best presents Garbo could give good friends was a special ear-protector, to use on aeroplanes, for example. Mimi Pollak is one of the people who received a couple of sets of this Garbo speciality.

But it was a serious matter to Garbo: she

204

suffered from being able to hear so much noise. I was able to discover for myself on one of our Alpine walks that even in the autumn of her years Garbo had perfect hearing. I could only catch part of what she could hear.

By now the letters from Hollywood were coming thick and fast.

On 31 May 1941 Garbo wrote to Hörke:

It seems so odd whenever I hear any-thing from home. You are the only person I hear from, so don't forget to put down a line or two in between the hours of book-keeping . . .

. . . As soon as it's possible, I'll be on my way over. I want to go up and sit on your roof and look out over to the Undsets'.

I'm still thinking about leaving, but then I get frightened again. Not of the ex-plosions at home, but of all the dreadful things going on at sea at the moment.

You won't forget to pray although it doesn't seem to help, will you. Tell Naj [Naima Wilfstrand], *dear little Naj, that she should help as well. Do give her a fond hug from me, please.*

Say hello to Sören [Wilhelm Sörensen] *as well and to everyone at Tistad.*

It seems as though being in touch with the family at Tistad became for Garbo more and more of an umbilical cord to Sweden.

Ninotchka was premièred in the USA on 9 November 1939. Garbo had nothing to do with any film studio for a whole year after that.

What follows is a couple of quotations from a letter dated 29 August 1940:

Dear Hörke, thank you for your letters. Now all I'm waiting for are the newspapers. Look what a go-getter I've become.

Sometimes when I let myself think about it, I get unbearably homesick. Best not to think about it . . .

. . . I haven't started working yet. But maybe I will in a 'while'. You never write about your sister and Yorkie's mother.

My life is much the same as usual, mostly on my own. Sometimes not on my own. Very rarely the latter.

I see My family once a week and the Nermans once a month, if that.

Quiet flows the river and yet is never still.

Darling Hörke, do write soon.

During the war the censors would even open private letters. It may be more than coincidence, if you are inclined to be suspicious, that the only one of Garbo's letters to Hörke that they opened was one in which she wrote about Axel Wenner-Gren.

In the autumn of 1989 Garbo was being discussed in a very delicate context. Sweden's ambassador to London, Leif Leifland, published a book intended to exonerate Axel Wenner-Gren, the industrial magnate, from the suspicion that he had worked for Hitler during the war: *Svartlistningen av Axel Wenner-Gren (The Blacklisting of Axel Wenner-Gren).*

The book lists documents from Allied intelligence organizations that were believed to prove that Garbo had been used as an agent in order to get inside information on what Wenner-Gren was up to. In common with David Niven and Noel Coward, she was supposed to have been made use of to get facts about the Swedish businessman's activities. Quite simply, Garbo was presented as a spy for the Allies.

I rang Garbo in New York and told her what I had read. At the same time I pointed out that it was bound to be seen as an honourable deed to have helped to find out information that led to the downfall of Hitler's Germany.

'I would have died of shame if I had ever had anything to do with spying.'

'But it is made clear you were on the right side . . .'

'That makes no difference. No one asked me to do anything like that. No, you can deny it, Mr Broman.'

Of course Garbo had met Axel Wenner-Gren, who loved being surrounded by celebrities. But according to Garbo her contacts with him were of a superficial nature.

Olof Lagercrantz tells a much saucier story about Garbo and Wenner-Gren, concerning a favourite experience of Bertil Malmberg, the writer and Academician:

'I saw Greta Garbo naked.'

Malmberg and Garbo and a few others were guests of the Wenner-Grens at Häringe Castle outside Stockholm. Early one morning after a late night, Malmberg saw Garbo from his window, walking on her own down to the deserted swimming-pool in the garden. Garbo took off all her clothes there and jumped naked into the water, little knowing she was being observed.

Maybe it was Bertil Malmberg who was the spy . . .

Below is the letter that was opened by the censors. As always it was important to Garbo that the picture of her presented in Sweden should be a proper one: 'I cherish my countrymen.'

December 1940
Hörke darling,
First let me say thanks for the papers. They make my homesickness worse but that doesn't matter . . .
. . . I'm telling you all this in the hope that it will be in time to be a Christmas greeting. You must be allowed to have your men home at Christmas otherwise it will just be too cruel . . .
. . . Nothing new on my part as usual. I've had a cold for over five months, so I haven't been very cheerful.
Just now I'm lying on a bench out in the desert all on my own. I'm the only

guest where I'm staying. I would love you to come and get me so we could travel to Sweden.

I was invited to our friends in Nassau, Axel W., but I can't travel. I'm off to New York soon for some kind of treatment. If it works you must come and have it too.

Then with God's help I'll start working again. They're in no hurry nowadays when our films are not being shown in Europe . . .

. . . God, if only we could sit in some little corner at Tistad and tell tales from the never-ending story.

Life could be so wonderful—if we only knew what to do with it.

We do so waste our time.

I'll never forget what Yorkie's mother said: 'It's a privilege to have been born.' . . .

. . . Take care my little friend and kiss Yorkie on one eye from me.

In her next letter Garbo wants help with an old life-insurance policy in Sweden:

5 February 1941
Dearest Hörke,

210

Thanks for your Christmas letter. Hope mine got there in time.

I have been in New York for a bit having treatment. I won't know whether it has helped until some time in the future.

Hörke darling, if you know how things will turn out, could you write to me on the following matter. I used to have a life-insurance policy in Sweden. We took out a loan on it since we didn't want to relinquish it—and brought the money over here. I have to pay a lot of interest on it. The latest thing over here is that it looks like foreigners 'financial assets will be frozen.

If I had the slightest inkling that Sweden would be safer I would send the money back. Do you know any way of finding out what would be the best thing to do? Though how anyone should know what to do these days, I don't know.

It's full of refugees over here and there's hardly any room. Poor people.

I can't get much out at the moment. Things are so hectic here.

I'm finding sleeping difficult. I feel like an invalid I'm so homesick for the countryside, for forests, lakes and for calm. For the old days or rather for the present but with the atmosphere of the old days.

It looks as though it will be several years before I'll be able to turn up at Tistad again. It's hard to think that way. But I suppose Heaven does have a plan in all this and there's nothing we can do.

I wish I were supernaturally strong so I could put right everything that is wrong. Instead I have to stay here and try to fix my messed-up body. If I get a lot fitter after this 'cure' I'll go and talk with 'Selassie'. I have no idea why.

Darling, do write whenever you've got a moment. You're my only link.

Say hello to Yorkie and Lasse [Gunnila]. *Take care. If you can do any-thing about my 'life'* [-insurance policy] *let me know as soon as you can.*
Love.

Garbo's mother, who was living in Santa Fe with her brother Sven and his family, was supposed to go home to Sweden in 1941, Garbo says in her next letter. But the war situation had deteriorated.

23 June 1941
Darling Hörke,
*Thanks for masses of papers and letters. I
do hope you'll get the coffee I'm sending
you someday . . .*

*. . . I've started work on a film, which
probably won't amount to much [Two-
Faced Woman].*

*In any event I don't feel too ashamed.
But these are such strange times that they
are worried that if it isn't a tiny bit vul-
gar it won't do well.*

*It's strange that I should be writing
about films when war is on our door-
step. Things look bad for Sweden once
more.*

*My family were supposed to go home
on 15 June on a Finnish boat, but no
boat turned up. And they were supposed to take some coffee home with
them.*

*How I would love to be able to talk
with you about masses of things. That
just can't happen.*

*Maybe the war will end soon. I do so
long to see you (and Larsson).*

*Have you got any thinner now there's
no coffee or is it the other way round for
you, Mrs Hörke?*

What month and on what date were you born? Can you believe I can't remember. Please let me know and I'll ask the stars if you're a nice girl.

Perhaps you haven't got time to write to me now. Maybe you will be feeling frightened and despairing when you get this . . .

. . . Your letters arrive unopened, so do tell me a little about what you think will happen. Love.

The next letter reveals more disappointment with *Two-Faced Woman*. And Garbo also mentions the problems caused by the shortage of coffee in Sweden during the war. Anyone with a foreign connection who could provide you with an extra ration was worth their weight in gold:

20 August 1941
Dearest Mrs Hörke,
Your letters always give me new hope.

I'll soon be finished with my latest baby [Two-Faced Woman] and have no idea what it will be like. Wonder when you'll get to see it. Don't even know if you can see films from over here like before.

I'm only very sorry that the story was changed so much. Salka [Viertel] had a much better 'story' to begin with. But since I would rather go walking in the country than fight for stories, it will have turned out like it has . . .

. . . Peg said she would try sending coffee and see if it arrived. Hope you got it. If it works I'll send more when I stop working.

Thank you for the picture of Losse [Gunnila]. She looks so nice and so capable and pretty. Tell her not to get married too quickly . . .

. . . Do you want me to send you film magazines, but sadly they are so stupid you probably won't want them.
Love.

Garbo gives the thumbs-down to *Two-Faced Woman* in a letter dated 24 October 1941. But more important things were happening. The USA was about to enter the war:

Dearest Hörke,
Thanks for letters and newspapers.
I am glad you've got the family at home with you. That always sounds more

hopeful. But I suppose they'll have to be off again. Have they got to go out into the cold again or is it good for the boys? I only know I want to be part of it.

I am looking for a house to buy but don't really want to. Though the rents are likely to rise so much that it would be stupid not to own your own home. But then you've got something to draw on.

I wonder if the taxes are as bad back home . . .

. . . Everyone is nervous and afraid.

I have finished with my 'latest' and sadly it's just nothing. Maybe you you'll see it soon and then you'll be able to see for yourself what's missing from my art. It was heartbreaking for Salka and me. But more important things are happening in the world, so I'd better stay silent. We're all afraid of being drawn into the war soon and then there there'll be panic.

It seems crazy that millions are being killed instead of a few thoughtful people getting together to try and sort out what's wrong. But then there would have to be give and take—and no one wants to give.

Hörke, how long will it be before we meet again? Maybe a few years. Or perhaps I could come and have dinner on *your 'cards' [ration cards].*

In that case we'll both be slim. But if you really pray hard every day, that will help. Otherwise I'll have to buy a house and a lot of other things I don't want.

The correspondence between Tistad and Garbo went on for almost twenty years. Then Garbo moved to New York and started travelling to Europe. The telephone became an ever more frequent instrument of communication.

All the friends Garbo brought with her to Sweden visited the Wachtmeisters at Tistad Castle, including George Schlee. In the area around Nyköping and by Lake Sillen people loved to say that they had caught a glimpse of the 'Divine One'. A remarkable number thought they remembered seeing Garbo dancing at the Huntsmen's Ball when it was held on Tistad's own open-air dance-floor. And there were even one or two who thought they remembered having danced the Schottische (a slow polka) with Garbo. Would that have been in 1937 or '38?

This is an undated letter from the war years:

Hörke darling,
Not a single word from you, what's the
matter? Don't you like me any more?
The last thing I heard from you was a
telegram . . .
. . . Nothing's happening as far as I am
concerned. I've still no children, nothing,
as usual.

The last few days here have been grey
and I have been thinking a lot about
Tistad. About summers there when it
rains and that marvellous melancholy en-
folds us . . .
. . . Maybe the war will end soon. Al-
though it would still be a good while
before travelling will be possible
again . . .
. . . Perhaps you don't want to go up
on the roof any more and look at the
fields.

At last the war ended. The first thing Garbo
planned on doing was visiting Sweden:

Beverly Hills, 5 June 1945
Darling Hörke,
When are you writing me a letter?
Spent my time chewing over whether to
go home in June or July. Would you

mind asking Grönlund at the Strand Hotel if there are any rooms available. Maybe Grönlund isn't even there any more . . .

. . . God knows what has been happening during all the years that have rushed by. Do ask, darling Mrs Hörke.

If they have nothing free there, maybe Max [Gumpel] knows of an apartment I could rent for a while. . . .

. . . I wonder how you and Yorkie are. Hope everything is well. It will be wondeful seeing you both again. I'm still in dirty old New York. Here's my new address:
904 North Bedford Drive
Beverly Hills
California

The next letter is part of film history. Garbo wrote in December 1945 that she was thinking of making a comeback. But at the same time she was worried that her appearance might have dimmed:

New York 16 December 1945
Darling Hörke,
It's Christmas once again. Yet another Christmas without Sweden. And time

is passing. How are you both? Is Yorkie all right now? If you only knew how often I have been thinking of you.

At present I am in New York. I'm living in an awful hotel and walk the streets, thinking about what it is like in Stockholm at this time of year. Dark at three o'clock. Which cheers me up dreadfully.

What's new, what has been happening? . . .

. . . I met the wife of one of the men on the America Line and she thought that the traffic would start again at the beginning of next year. I'll be coming then.

Before that maybe you could write and tell me more about yourself and things at home. It would be so wonderful to get letters from you at Christmas. Maybe I'll get one . . .

. . . I have been considering a film I might try making, but I don't know. Time leaves its traces on our small faces and bodies. And it's not the same any more, being able to pull it off.

So I was wondering about whether I should or not. At present only 'our father in heaven' knows whether it will come off.

I hope that science will discover something to help us, so that we're not left with no help at all. Although I don't see how the world would work if we all had eternal youth.

I have no idea how I would arrange the world if I had the power to do so . . .

. . . I am still just as lonely. Nothing changes. I spend my time wondering why I don't have some marvellous person to go around with and look at all the bits and pieces they have nowadays. But I have got no one. And so it goes.

Hörke, my sweetheart, pick up paper and pen at once and write to me . . .
Love to you both.

The long years of war changed the lives and plans of many people. Garbo stayed, more or less against her will, in the USA and acquired a residence of a more permanent kind.

New York
6 February 1946
Dearest, darling Hörke,
I am wondering once more why we never

221

write. Maybe you're going through the same feelings as I am at present. Or maybe you're still the same, old cheerful Hörke.

It can't be all that long now before we meet again. I heard that the Boströms [the Swedish ambassador in Washington] *are going to Sweden in August. Of course I don't know that you really want to see me. I hope so anyway. May I come straight to you? . . .*

I have bought a home here after all these years and am trying to furnish the blessed nuisance, and it's not easy. Everything I do is wrong. I have never worked as hard as I am doing now. And nothing happens.

I am the head gardener as well. My hands are getting ruined and so I put cream on them at night and ruin them again the next day. Crazy as usual . . .

. . . I wonder if Larsson is still with you. And whether you have got any calves. I don't suppose you'll be able to keep them much longer.

Is it difficult getting food or will you be able to manage to feed us when I come? . . .

. . . I have been in New York for several months. I had a little accident down here so I just left everything and went to live in the big city for a while.

I have tried to get away from this place so often because I will never work again at my former job. And I don't think I want to be a gardener other than when needs must . . .

. . . . I'm still living quietly and away from it all, so I've nothing exciting to tell you about. I'll just have to wait for your letter and you know how heavy time weighs on those who wait. So please Hörke write when you can otherwise I won't be able to travel to see you. (Threat!)

Do give yourself and Yorkie a hug from me and I'll soon be over in Boström's suitcase. Love.

In 1960 Gunnila Wachtmeister visited New York and went to see Garbo, who took Lasse—as she still called her—on a tour of Manhattan. Garbo was under the impression that there was a shortage of almost everything in Sweden and dragged Gunnila off to a boutique where she immediately purchased three dozen pairs of nylon stockings to send to Hörke as a present. Gunnila did not have the heart to tell her that by then you could get most things in Swedish shops as well.

In 1962 Garbo went to see the Wachtmeisters in Stockholm. Count Nils Wachtmeister had by then been dead for two years. Garbo suddenly turned up at the Märta School in Birger Jarl's Street, where Gunnila Wachtmeister, now Mrs Bussler, was the principal. There were lots of hugs and kisses.

The following day Gunnila drove Garbo down in her little Fiat to Södermanland to see Hörke, who had moved from the castle and was living on the Lunds' estate.

Hörke Wachtmeister, who was ten years older than Garbo, died in 1977. When Garbo heard the news she wrote a letter of condolence to Gunnila with the help of someone who used a typewriter with a typestyle that was reminiscent of handwriting.

A younger relative, Ebba Wachtmeister, was also there during Garbo's visit. She used to call Hörke, Granny. 'You shouldn't say that,' said Garbo. 'It sounds so old. You should call her Hörke.'

In Klosters I could not help mentioning

that the widowed Gunnila Wachtmeister had remarried, to a widower, Carl Johan Bernadotte.

'I approve. Carl Johan Bernadotte is a real gentleman,' said Garbo.

13

'It Feels Like A Piece
Of Sweden To Me'

Garbo knew the whole canton of Grau-bünden—Klosters, Klosters Dorf Wolf-gang, Davos, Flüela and all the other places —from end to end; all at a height of 1400 metres or more. She had been walking there for almost thirty years, often on her own, along footpaths and Alpine trails.

She was known to remark with satisfaction that the coat of arms of Graubünden was in blue and yellow: 'They have the Swedish national colours here.'

But Garbo's favourite place of all—her paradise on earth, you could say—was Monstein, a very small Alpine village, 1624 metres above sea level and roughly ten kilometres south of Davos. We drove there with Garbo on two occasions, in 1986 and 1987.

Some of the farmers in Monstein make a living by keeping cattle that graze on the steep slopes. Monstein is also a starting-point for walking-tours of the mountains and comes to life in summertime. The area is surrounded by snow-clad Alpine peaks.

As a result of a great deal of asking for directions we finally found the right track. Garbo was totally lacking in any sense of direction and would often point out the wrong way. But—she was good at asking questions and would be constantly telling me, the driver, to pull up. She would wind down the passenger-seat window and ask one person after another for directions.

One lady described the route we should follow in a dialect of Swiss German I found difficult to understand and she was so intent on being helpful she almost ended up inside the car. She suddenly started staring at Garbo and said: 'Oh, it's you. You must let me ask you for an autograph for my children.'

'Thank you very much,' replied Garbo politely, wound up the window and said, 'Drive on, Mr Broman.'

The last bit of the road to Monstein was under construction and so narrow that cars could not pass one another. You had to drive along the edge of a precipice—without a kerb. I could hardly bear to look down for fear of becoming dizzy. That was when I discovered that Garbo had no fear of heights. Sheer drops had no effect on her whatsoever.

Although Monstein consisted only of a few farms, its original church had become too small and was then being used as a grain store and as a venue for minor musical events. A new church was built on a slope with a magnificent view over the valley. Garbo, my wife and I walked into the open and quite empty church.

The interior was in wood, rather Spartan but friendly, and smelt freshly polished. Garbo told us she had sat there many times over the years. In the chapel there stood a little table covered with a simple cloth in a cross-stitch pattern. A bowl of water containing a bunch of Alpine flowers adorned the table. There was a smell of wood—a good, clean smell.

I stepped up to the pulpit and looked out over the entire congregation: Greta Garbo and my wife sitting on the front bench. I could not resist the pleasure of reminding them of the opening words of *Gösta Berlings Saga*, the film in which Garbo made her breakthrough.

'At last the priest was standing at the pulpit,' I began . . .

'Bravo, bravo,' Garbo said rather loudly, and clapped her hands.

Outside the church was a tiny little cemetery with simple, solid wooden crosses and a few humble gravestones.

'Well, you have to be prepared for that, too,' Garbo sighed. 'But I want to lie in Swedish soil.'

Garbo invited us to lunch at an inn in Monstein. She was dieting and hardly ate anything. We had cheese for dessert, 'Monk's crown', Garbo's favourite cheese. She cut it up into small cubes herself and offered it to us.

She paid and left a generous tip. 'I have never owned a credit card.'

Garbo came to Klosters in the sixties on the recommendation of her friend Salka Viertel. For the first few years she hired a flat close to Salka, who liked to hold open house just like in Hollywood. In later years, as her health became a problem, Salka used to have her dinner prepared by the Hotel Pardenn and sent over. Garbo used the same service at her flat.

Lucienne Graessli, who ran the hotel,

would often bring the trays over herself. At Salka's she would ring before entering and then place the tray on the dining table. She would also ring the bell at Garbo's door but as requested would leave the tray on the floor just outside.

People came to Klosters from all over the world, including many from America. At the end of the sixties, a New York couple, Mr and Mrs Friedländer, started spending several weeks each summer in Klosters. Lotte Friedländer remembered that as a girl in Vienna she had had a piano teacher called Viertel, who was Salka's brother. This led to a friendship that was to last for many years. It was at Salka's that Mrs Friedländer got to know Garbo. When Salka's health deteriorated—she died in 1978—she urged Mrs Friedländer: 'Take good care of Greta.'

In many of the pictures from Klosters in recent years that have been shown in the press, standing supportively at Garbo's side is Lotte Friedländer. Her husband, a businessman who died a year or two ago, used to deal with Garbo's fan mail in Klosters. 'He enjoys doing that kind of thing,' said Garbo.

The stamps on the envelopes would be

passed on by Mr Friedländer to the then manager of the hotel, who used to collect them.

'Every Christmas in New York I used to bake a special Austrian cake for Garbo that she liked,' said Mrs Friedländer. 'But Garbo was so ill during the Christmas of 1989 that we couldn't meet. The Christmas before, Garbo gave me a lovely Baroque angel as a Christmas present. We used to speak on the telephone once a week. Gigi, as I used to call her, went downhill very rapidly. Only a few years ago she was so vital and fit that I used to find it difficult keeping up with her.'

The hotel staff were impressive in the way they sought to protect Garbo. All the employees seemed to be unbribable.

'But then we do have some experience of celebrities,' the hotel owner, Lucienne Graessli, insists. 'Immediately after the war a single gentleman arrived from Paris—Ernest Hemingway. He was given room number 411, next door, incidentally, to room number 410, where Garbo stayed over so many years.

'I was at reception when Hemingway registered as Mr Greenburg. I couldn't help looking him straight in the eye and asking,

"Is that the right name?" Hemingway smiled, winked and said, "I don't think you want to be nosy or inquisitive, do you, Miss . . . ?"

'Elisabeth Bergner, the actress, used to stay here for long periods, as well. And a year or so ago, Lady Di, Princess Diana, came for the day and went swimming in our indoor pool.

'There were periods when Garbo kept to her room, when she wasn't feeling well. Sometimes she would just pick at her food. I asked her when she seemed to have no appetite if there was anything she would like. We were prepared to give her whatever we could. Garbo looked cautiously, almost shyly at me and said, "Well, what I'd like would be Russian caviar and vodka." That is what she got.'

'The last time Garbo stayed at the hotel she was very frail and weak. Her doctor in New York flew over together with Garbo's niece, Mrs Gray Reisfield, and took her home. That was the first time she kissed me on both cheeks, when she said goodbye. She had never done that before. It was like a last goodbye . . .

'Garbo was an easygoing guest but she was totally solitary. The first few years she would start the day by doing exercises on the hotel veranda, often together with Mrs Friedländer. Garbo wasn't the slightest bit shy in safe surroundings.'

Garbo had never set foot in the rustic bar of the hotel before my wife and I led her into temptation. The bar was as good as empty mostly but became remarkably popular when Garbo was sitting there: 'They're only coming here to have a drink so they can get a look at me,' said Garbo, who knew what to expect from them.

We provided Garbo with Swedish newspapers during our visit.

One day she had been reading about Sweden's economy in *Dagens Nyheter,* a positive article about the finance minister, Kjell-Olof Feldt. 'Let's drink to Sweden's minister of finance, then,' said a cheerful Garbo, who was pleased when things were looking up for Sweden.

'Whenever I pass the parking lot, I usually give your car a pat, Mr Broman. It feels like a piece of Sweden to me.

Garbo came into our hotel room one day— 'They haven't finished cleaning my room yet'—and sat down and said: 'You must naturally think I'm a very spoilt person—which I am, of course. But it's so nice to be able to speak Swedish—I never get the chance in New York.'

She nestled into her armchair, kicked off her slipper-like shoes and said, 'My feet always hurt. And I've bought myself so many shoes that when you come and see me at my home in New York, Mrs Broman will be welcome to a few pairs.'

Garbo's feet were thin. Her legs were slim—the little you could see of them under her long trousers. According to Mimi Pollak, Garbo used to practise walking on tiptoe to make her legs slimmer during her studies at the Royal Dramatic Theatre stage school.

A couple of times Garbo took us with her to the Bally shoe store in Davos where she had been personally acquainted with the manager, Glan Pedermann, for many years. She always asked him to remember her to his wife. Garbo told him she did not want any shoes for herself but had come along to help my wife and me choose shoes.

Garbo suddenly asked, 'Have you heard the story about the man who went to see a psychiatrist because he was feeling so depressed? The doctor talked with the patient for a bit and then made a suggestion: "You have to have a good laugh now and then. There is a circus in town at the moment that's got a very funny clown. All the punters laugh at him. You should go there one evening."

' "I can't do that. I'm the clown . . ." '

Of course we never got to know Garbo intimately. She would say, 'I'm fed up with myself for not having fixed things up for myself better. It's too late now.

She was very matter-of-fact in a rather impressive way, she had a straightforward way of putting things that was not bitter but simply: that's how it is. Her eyes were clear and penetrating.

When we talked about Sweden I could not help mentioning to her that the familiar form of address, *'du'*, was almost universally used nowadays and it was rather unusual to use the formal *'ni'* or use the third person form of address.

'So there's no need to call me "sir", madam.'

It was not really my intention that we should abandon the formal form of address when talking to one another. I just wanted to give Garbo the opportunity of making things a bit simpler.

'Not on your life,' said Garbo cheerily. 'I tried to do it a couple of years ago with the writer, John Gunther, whom I often used to meet together with his wife in New York. She is still one of my best friends. Once when I popped by, John Gunther was sitting as usual at his typewriter. "Hi there, Johnny," I said and patted him on the back.

'He was absolutely appalled and we decided to continue addressing one another as we had always done. I called him Mr Gunther.'

Garbo was quite capable of letting you know what she thought. Although she thought journalists were the lowest form of life, she obviously continued to read those rotten newspapers. One day she told me, delighting in her own sense of mischief, that the hotel manager had shown her a German newspaper that reported that Garbo was about to get married. 'It's never too late, Mr Broman—I'm still a going proposition,' she giggled with pleasure.

Garbo had an old-fashioned way, a very nice way, of saying goodbye that was both kindly and considerate. It was very important to her that we should tell her explicitly when we were leaving. It was taken for granted that she would then come down from her room, say goodbye properly, embrace us both and then stand there waving to us as we left. This brought tears to my wife's and my eyes every time—and to Garbo's as well.

14

'I've Been To Napoleon's Tomb More Than Thirty Times'

One of the things Garbo was most interested in doing was wandering round churchyards. Most often she would do it on her own. This may all have started because she wanted a definite goal when she was out walking or she may just have wanted somewhere to relax during her walks.

It was at Garbo's prompting that we came to visit three churchyards in Klosters and Davos. 'There are more of them around here, but we'll have to visit them another time,' she said.

The first cemetery that Garbo took us to can be found right beside one of the hospitals in Davos—Wolfgang Hochgebirg's clinic, a specialist unit for asthma patients. The hospital used to be called the German

Clinic of Davos and used to care primarily for consumptives.

There is a very discreetly located cemetery on a wooded slope beside the hospital, sheltered by tall conifers: the *Soldatenfriedhof*, the soldiers' cemetery. This is the last resting-place of German soldiers from the First World War. They had tuberculosis and were sent from the war to this sanatorium, where many of them died.

Garbo pointed out a simple monument bearing the legend (in German):

German soldiers lie here in peace, the
   guests of strangers,
Far from home they, too, died for the
   Fatherland.

Simple crosses stand next to tall fir trees that make the cemetery seem so well hidden that you can almost walk past it without seeing the gravestones. Garbo pointed out how young many of the soldiers who had died of TB far from their homeland had been. There were no flowers on any of the graves.

The next day Garbo took us to the cemetery used by the inhabitants of Davos, the Wiltboden Forest Cemetery, on a hill at the edge of the town. This public cemetery is more representative of the smaller Alpine communities: neat gravestones, many wooden crosses, a lot of flowers. It, too, was located in a wood—there was silence apart from the tranquil sound of the wind in the firs and the pines.

There are several small cemeteries in Klosters and its surroundings. In the centre of Klosters is the Evangelische (Protestant) church with a tiny cemetery that positively glows with an abundance of flowers. The people who take care of the cemetery make sure that every grave always has fresh flowers—it is a lovely sight.

It was there that we stopped beside Salka Viertel's beautifully simple gravestone, with its inscription:

Salka Viertel
1888–1978

Salka had been Garbo's friend since they met in Hollywood in 1929. She had helped to write several of Garbo's films. Salka had a son who has a home in Klosters—the writer Peter Viertel, who is married to the English actress, Deborah Kerr—although they live in Spain for the most part.

Between making these trips Garbo told us that she—who sadly felt unable to believe and lacked any certainty about what happened to people when they die—found a sort of peace in wandering around church-yards.

A friend of hers had told her that in Los Angeles it was difficult to find peace even in the cemeteries. Natalie Wood's grave, so Garbo was told, lay so close to a motorway that visitors to the grave were deafened.

Garbo's favourite grave-site—'to which I always return'—was the tomb of Napoleon in Paris. 'You must think I'm crazy, but I've been to Napoleon's tomb more than thirty times,' she told us. 'I am not a great fan of Napoleon, but I think it is the most remarkable grave-site in the world. I have never missed the chance to go there when I've been in Paris.'

'Was your interest stimulated while you were filming *Conquest* and you were playing opposite Napoleon [Charles Boyer]?'

'No, you mustn't confuse what happens in film studios with reality, Mr Broman. I hadn't seen Napoleon's tomb then and I knew hardly anything about him.

'No, I have done a lot of walking in Paris, up and down its streets, and that's when

I discovered that it's always cool at Napoleon's tomb. But that's not why I go there.

'I do wonder whether they couldn't have made a smaller coffin so that the whole thing didn't seem so pompous. But still . . . for me Napoleon was a solitary person, who in the midst of all the madness tried to do good for his country.'

'I don't feel a bit like Napoleon and I loathe all war—don't think I'm mad . . . But I still like visiting the tomb at the Invalides. There is always a screaming flock of schoolchildren around you, and yet at the same time there is a stillness there that I cannot explain and that I've never found anywhere else.

'Not that I understand the French at all. First of all they exile Napoleon to a desolate island where he is supposed to die, cut off from all honour and decency. And then they bring him home and allot him a place accorded to no other person of any country. There is a whole temple built around Napoleon's tomb.

'Nor can I help being fascinated by Napoleon's life. He seems to me to have been a very much misunderstood person. But then for that matter I don't idolize anyone.

Garbo was very concerned that we should not get the idea that she suffered from delusions of grandeur or that she had a Napoleon complex or any kind of screw loose.

Garbo's wonder is surely well-founded, for in that sarcophagus, which incidentally includes another six coffins made of various materials, there lie the mortal remains of a man who was in the end banished and died in exile on Saint Helena in 1821.

The sarcophagus, which stands on a plinth of green granite from the Vosges, is in the Empire style. It was made in red porphyry from—Finland! Around the walls of the tomb stand twelve goddesses of victory and some marble reliefs depicting the victories of Napoleon.

Over the entrance is an inscription, which is a quotation from Napoleon's will:

It is my wish that my remains be allowed to rest by the banks of the Seine amidst the people of France whom I loved so dearly.

Napoleon died in 1821. His remains were placed in the Invalides in 1840, where they have since remained.

As we wandered with Garbo around

those cemeteries in the Alps I sometimes got a sense that what she needed was the feeling of reverence, of the devotional—that was where she could finally be at peace.

'Not that I've made any preparations for all this,' she once sighed in the little cemetery in Monstein. She went on, though, not talking directly to my wife or me, 'But I want to be buried in Sweden. I want to go home to Sweden . . .,

Garbo was able to speak about the most sensitive matters in a cool and matter-of-fact way. It was as though she wanted to conjure up peace and quiet.

'There are Jewish graves here, you know, where they place small stones on the graves. There's nothing that gives you such a feeling for the eternal as wandering around a churchyard. It's not at all macabre. It is very peaceful.'

15

'Churchill Urged Me To Make A Come-Back'

In the autumn of 1986 Garbo was awarded the Illis Quorum by the Swedish government. This mark of distinction was presented to her in New York by the Swedish ambassador in Washington, Wilhelm Wachtmeister, who was accompanied by his wife.

'The award ceremony took place at my friend Jane Gunther's, who is much better than I am at arranging receptions,' Garbo told me proudly. 'The ambassador made a speech and it was all very grand. I felt very honoured.'

When I heard about the award I sent Garbo a postcard to congratulate her and wrote: 'Now there is only the Nobel prize left.'

Garbo had received almost all the Swedish medals and honours anyone can get. When we met a while later the first thing she said was: 'Your postcard about "Now there is only the Nobel prize left" was the most amusing post I got all year, Mr Broman.'

Garbo returned to it several times, which I naturally found very gratifying. She touted what I had said about the Nobel prize to such an extent that there were moments when I thought she had taken the whole matter more seriously than I intended. But Garbo loved making jokes.

'As you know, there is no Nobel prize for actors, so it would have to be the Peace prize in this case. Well, your films have made people happy all over the world, brought people together . . . and that's the way to create peace, isn't it?'

Of course, all this was idle chatter, but we touched on troublesome events in the world as well and Garbo praised Gorbachev for succeeding in having a humanizing effect on society in the East.

'He is someone I'd like to meet,' said Garbo. 'Couldn't you arrange for us to travel to Moscow, Mr Broman . . . You know that in America we call him Gorby . . . Garbo and Gorby discuss peace . . .'

Unable to give her the Nobel prize, I wanted to be a bit grand and give Garbo something out of the ordinary—one of the stars in the sky. You can buy one from a Canadian firm that is part of an organization that exists to gather funds for an observatory.

Garbo was sitting in our hotel room in Klosters. I explained that many of the stars in the sky lack names, but I had arranged for one of them to be known as Greta Garbo from now on.

'That'll have to be the Star of Bethlehem, then,' Garbo joked.

'I'm afraid that one's already taken, but I've got the certificate here.'

I then produced the special star chart that I had had sent to me with all the related documents, etc.

The star known as Greta Garbo is a sun one hundred times larger than the sun of our solar system and can be found just next to the pole star—only it's infinitely further away.

Garbo folded together all the paraphernalia and then said quietly: 'Thank you. I promise to continue shining over everything, good as well as bad, in the future as well.'

Garbo had met them all: 'I once flew from

New York to Los Angeles and happened to sit next to a sporting celebrity who had been married to Marilyn Monroe—Joe DiMaggio.

'Just as we were approaching California a terrible thunderstorm burst upon us. The plane tumbled this way and that. I was terrified. I couldn't help putting my hand in Joe DiMaggio's then. I didn't know him at all, but he was kind to me and took good care of me and I felt a lot safer with his support.

'We were forced to land at a back-up airport because of the storm. There were very few taxis there and there were a lot of people on the plane. But Joe DiMaggio was famous and an idol and he got a taxi straight away. He asked me if I wanted a lift and took me where I wanted to go. A real gentleman.'

On the subject of flying, Garbo told me about another long flight when she sat next to a gentleman who had drunk a good deal and then fallen asleep. In his sleep he happened to lean his head against Garbo's shoulder, which she found a bit of a bother. He also snored.

'I tried calmly to get him into an upright position. Then, when he woke up, he stared at me and said in astonishment: "Oh, it's you, is it?" Then he went straight back to sleep.

Garbo always appeared in trousers. There was, however, one occasion on which she departed from her custom. That was when she was invited to dinner with President John F. Kennedy at the White House.

'That was a rather formal event and friends of mine who knew what those things were like recommended that I wear a skirt,' she told me.

'It was a lovely, intimate dinner: just the president and his wife Jackie, plus a gentleman from New York and myself.' (The man was Lem Billings, a businessman who had been at school with Kennedy and was an old friend of the family.)

'President Kennedy did not smoke and drank only water,' Garbo explained. 'I felt like one of the damned when I lit a cigarette.

'He asked me what I was doing—this was in 1962—and I answered that I was a collector. What was I supposed to say?

' "What do you collect?" Kennedy asked.

' "Here's an example," I said and opened my handbag to show him an article I had torn out of a magazine, which was about Kennedy.

'The president looked at me in surprise. Then he asked me what my thoughts were about a particular political issue that was then current and up for discussion in the Congress, to allow abortions or not. What did I think about that issue?'

There was no doubt that Garbo was very flattered by the invitation even though she felt a little out of her depth.

I could not help but ask the classic question: 'How did you find out about Kennedy's death?'

'I was sitting watching television. It was Walter Cronkite who announced the dreadful thing that had occurred. And I thought I could see tears in his eyes . . .

Then there was Onassis.

'During my years on the Riviera I met Onassis a great many times, and his cousin Niarchos as well. In his youth Onassis had attended a school in Gothenburg that had something to do with shipping. He spoke little Swedish. He called me "Vackra svenska flicka" [Beautiful Swedish girl].

'On board the yacht *Christina* he even had a huge swimming-pool. Onassis loved practical jokes and I was there when he shoved Niarchos and some other people who were fully dressed into the pool. Oh, how he laughed. He didn't dare have a go at me.

'Once when sailing in *Christina* we went ashore and the whole company set off to find a bar. Both Onassis and Niarchos had pea-shooters with them and started shooting at the lovely plates that had been hung on the bar's walls. They were all smashed and the pieces littered the floor. Onassis just took out his wallet and paid for all the devastation. No, I was not amused.'

'I met Winston Churchill several times while staying on the Riviera, mostly through Onassis. Churchill couldn't understand why I stopped filming, and urged me to make a come-back. He felt I should start working again the very next day.

' "It's never too late," he said. "Look at me, I didn't become Prime Minister until I was over fifty years old and I had to fight a World War." '

Long after Garbo told me about Churchill, I was reading an article in *Svenska Dagbladet* (a 'quality' Swedish daily newspaper) by Kerstin Hallert that recounted a story from a book of memoirs by the grandson of Winston Churchill. During lunch with Churchill and others Garbo was supposed to have removed her woollen trousers. I could not help but ring Garbo and tell her what I had just read.

'At last, words of truth in a newspaper,' Garbo said, laughing. 'Yes, that's quite right, but it wasn't as bad as it sounds. We were having lunch at the Château Madrid restaurant in the mountains above Monaco.

'Onassis and Churchill were there and so was Clementine, so you needn't think anything untoward, Mr Broman. It was sunny and got so incredibly hot . . . and I had on an extra pair of woollen slacks that I wriggled out of under the table. Are they really writing about things like that now?

'Churchill was very interesting, but he only wanted to talk about war. He offered me a cigar. But I declined. A woman can hardly smoke a cigar. But I do regret that. I could have had one of Winston Churchill's cigars.'

Another Nobel laureate Garbo was pleased to have met was Selma Lagerlöf

'I was very nervous about meeting her,' Garbo explained. 'Selma Lagerlöf had asked for a chance to meet me when I was home from Hollywood sometime in the thirties. The meeting took place at the house of a friend [Valborg Olander] in Karla Street. I went there together with my friend Einar Nerman, but he had to wait at the entrance.

'We sat in a lovely drawing-room and Selma Lagerlöf thanked me for my work in *Gösta Berlings Saga* and she praised Mauritz Stiller.

'I was very nervous but Selma had a very calming effect on me. She also had very warm and lovely eyes. She had heard that the press was paying an awful lot of attention to me and that I was scared of journalists. Like many others she thought I would deal with it all much better if I were to meet the press halfway. "It's not much fun when the press ignore you to death either," said Selma.

'But Selma Lagerlöf had no idea what things were like in America. I really did my best to make myself available. I wasn't so stupid that I couldn't see that publicity was sometimes necessary for a film and its actors. But what usually happened in America was that they simply invented things—whether I had spoken to them or not.

'I was impressed by how modern Selma Lagerlöf was. She spoke very well about film as an art-form and wanted me to get film companies interested in several of her books.'

At some point in the fifties, Garbo got to know the Aga Khan. An affection developed, though it was one-sided: the Aga Khan was keen, Garbo reluctant. She was not interested.

Sir Michael Duff, an Englishman who could not perhaps match the Aga Khan in terms of wealth but was hardly a pauper, described some of the details of the story of how the Aga Khan did his courting. Sir Michael was a cheerful and generous host at the large-scale social events he arranged and it was not at all unusual to see thirty or forty Rolls-Royces all at the same time in the parking area when he had a party at his mansion in North Wales.

He was a great dance enthusiast and in order to learn the latest steps would hire Fred Astaire and Ginger Rogers, for example, and fetch them over by plane from Hollywood. The Englishman had met and got to know Garbo in New York.

Garbo tired of all the pearl necklaces, jewels, diamond bracelets and so on that the Aga Khan sent her. She made her resolution, shoved the whole caboodle into an envelope, stuck it down and sent the lot off by post to the Aga Khan.

There are women who do support themselves.

The Broadway star Mary Martin used to live for a while in the same building in Manhattan as Garbo. Her son Larry Hagman —alias 'J. R.' in *Dallas*—used to come and see his mother now and then, and one time Garbo was paying a visit. 'We saw a happy and open Garbo who was very talkative,' he told me in Stockholm.

A year or so ago MGM was sold to Ted Turner, the Texas TV tycoon. His principal interest was in acquiring all the old MGM films—those of Garbo, *Gone with the Wind* etc.—to show them on television round the world.

MGM's studios in Culver City were acquired by Columbia. For reasons of piety Columbia have kept the old names of two of the largest studio buildings—the Greta Garbo Building and the Katharine Hepburn Building.

The Garbo Building—the only building in the world to bear her name—was transformed into offices for the production of *Dallas*. Larry Hagman's dressing-room was on the ground floor.

16

'No One Is Ever Allowed In Here'

The high point of our friendship with Garbo was when my wife and I were invited to visit her at her home in New York. This was on 8 December 1987.

We had arrived in New York on the sixth, which was a Sunday, and had immediately announced our arrival to Garbo by sending her some flowers. We were staying at the Hotel St Moritz on 59th Street and had a view over Central Park.

Early Monday morning, Garbo rang to welcome us. 'We must meet,' she said. 'I stayed at the St Moritz as well, a long while back. They used to have an awful journalist living there whose name was Walter Winchell. He wrote in his column that he had been into my room . . . He was never in my room.'

'Well,' I said, 'the hotel has no doubt seen better days, but we've got a nice view and isn't it unusually sunny and warm for this time of year? At home they'll be crowning Santa Lucia at Skansen on Sunday and the day after tomorrow the king will be distributing all the Nobel prizes . . .'

'Really? I was Lucia once, you know. It was in Hollywood with Salka Viertel's family. I got to play Lucia and to hand out the Christmas presents.

Garbo was in a very sunny mood. This was a good omen.

She rang again. We were invited to come and see her at four p.m. on Tuesday. 'And no one is ever allowed in here, you know.'

I can remember a conversation with Garbo in Klosters. She was talking about her apartment in New York and her works of art.

'Have you read anything by Truman Capote, Mr Broman?'

'Well yes, I understand what you are referring to. I must say I was very upset on your behalf.'

Truman Capote had written that Garbo knew no better than to hang a picture by Picasso upside down.

'Capote has never been in my apartment.'

Garbo was obviously indignant.

She had given us prior warning about her paintings.

'I have eight pictures that my home help finds hard to take—she's actually afraid to dust those paintings. They are eight portraits by Jawlensky.'

By then, I had had a chance to read up on him: Alexei von Jawlensky (1864–1941) was a German painter of Russian birth. He worked in Munich, where he belonged to the group of artists known as 'Der Blaue Reiter'. He used dark, glowing colours and painted still lifes and portraits, notable for their icon-like stylization and their melancholic and mysterious character.

An art dealer said that Jawlensky's portraits sold for between 600,000 and one million kronor—£60,000–£100,000— apiece.

My wife and I were all neat and spruced up and had fifteen yellow roses with us when we arrived promptly at four p.m. at 450 East 52nd Street. An elderly, rather grizzled, short and plump doorman in a dark-green uniform jacket gave us a very friendly welcome at the entrance. I informed him we were going to see Miss Garbo. We were clearly expected, since this news did not seem to surprise him.

The doorman opened the door to one of the spacious lifts. He went up with us and pressed the button for the fifth floor. We stepped out of the lift and entered a little room, a sort of ante-chamber. There was a small painting of birds adorning one wall —this was somewhat reminiscent of an English hunting motif.

We rang the bell. The door opened at once and there stood Greta Garbo and her home help, a lady of the same age.

'Welcome to my home,' Garbo said and smiled like a ray of sunshine.

I gave her a big hug, as she stood there wearing the beige slacks and a beige polo-neck sweater that I had often seen in Klosters, with her long grey-white hair.

We said hello to 'my home help', who stood there decorously bending forward at Garbo's side. She had white hair and was dressed in a black waitress outfit with a white apron.

'You know, no one comes here,' Garbo said and showed us through a corridor into a large drawing-room. I was immediately struck by how large the room was, but it was all lovely, harmonious and cosy.

'This is always shut up. No one ever sets foot in here,' Garbo emphasized.

The large drawing-room was L-shaped with huge windows looking on to the East River. There was a glass door standing open to a balcony overlooking the river. We did not get the impression at all that this room was usually shut up. The air was fresh and the whole drawing-room felt that way.

On the coffee table stood a dish with cheese sandwiches, and some with other toppings and fillings, nuts, Russian vodka, Martini, whisky . . .

Garbo showed us round.

We went out on to the balcony, where we had an extensive view over the East River and Long Island. Far below us heavy traffic moved along East River Drive. I almost got vertigo looking down. But Garbo, her walking-stick in her hand, leant calmly against the apparently fragile parapet and pointed with her stick. Just as during our motoring tours in Switzerland, she had no fear of heights, she did not suffer from vertigo.

The drawing-room was generously proportioned and contained sofas, tables and chairs, a writing desk, vases and various ornamental objects. But there was not a single framed photograph. There was nothing personal in that sense.

Garbo sat down in an armchair and invited us to sit. I got the job of mixing the drinks for everyone.

Almost a whole wall was taken up with bookshelves, holding only bound books. I went over and looked at the authors' names: Thackeray, Shakespeare . . .

'I haven't read them,' said Garbo.

I looked in vain for a Renoir that I had heard Garbo owned. But I could not avoid seeing all those Jawlensky portraits she had told me about. It was hard not to feel some sympathy for the home help, who was, according to Garbo, afraid of the pictures; intense, large dark eyes stared at you wherever you turned. I saw it as a warning signal: Keep a grip on yourself. You are being watched. It was as though Garbo was keeping a vicarious eye on the gathering even when she was not there.

Garbo was tired but not yet disabled in her legs as she would come to be six months later.

'Now, I'd like to see your Oscar,' I said.

We had discussed it earlier. And Garbo quickly produced a box from under the bookshelves from which she took out the glittering golden object. It was taller and heavier than I expected. Tears almost came to my eyes as I stood there holding that heavy statuette inscribed:

Greta Garbo
For her unforgettable screen
performances
1954

'I do think this award should stand here on the writing table,' I said.

Garbo was actually moved by my reaction and exclaimed:

'So you're not ashamed of me in Sweden, then?'

'No, we're very proud of you.'

'When all that was going on, they rang from Hollywood, you know—they wanted me to go and fetch it in person at that gala of theirs,' said Garbo. 'I did not want to. Then they suggested that they interview me on the telephone during the broadcast, but I declined. It was the wife of my old agent who went to pick the object up and I think she had it for two years before it ended up here.

I was afraid Garbo would put the Oscar back in its box as soon as we left, but it stood majestically on the writing table the whole time we were there. (It was with pleasure that I learnt that the piece was still standing on top of the writing table a year later.)

'Oh yes, next year the king and queen want to meet me, you know. You must come over then and give me a hand.'

Garbo had been contacted prior to the Delaware Jubileum in 1988. 'I've no idea what to do,' she said. 'If it had been twenty years ago . . .

A painting that Garbo gave particular prominence to was a large, modern, non-figurative, almost square painting that hung over one of the sofas. It was obvious that it was relatively new and had been selected by Garbo herself.

There were a number of carpets of various shapes and sizes on top of the fitted carpet. They helped to make the room quiet and restful despite the apartment's location in the centre of Manhattan.

The home help left and Garbo herself went into the large kitchen a couple of times to butter some more biscuits. I tucked in and had no intention of leaving this lavish and unique festivity in a hurry.

That autumn Ingmar Berman's memoirs, *The Magic Lantern,* had been published and we discovered 'that Garbo had already read the book. What did she think of it?

She was thrilled by it. Garbo had visited Ingmar Bergman at the Råsunda film studios at the beginning of the sixties and he devoted a whole page of the book to his meeting with her. His description of Garbo ended with his opinion that she had an ugly mouth. To make doubly sure, he had had a detailed look at several Garbo films in which he believed he had found evidence for this idea: there *was* something funny about Garbo's mouth.

Everyone has described Garbo as divine, as perfect of form, a woman whose beauty was immaculate, and so on.

I asked her what she thought of Ingmar Bergman's book.

'It's quite superb,' she pronounced her verdict with conviction.

'But he didn't exactly like your mouth, did he?'

I tried to provoke her a little.

'Pooh! He can think what he likes.' Garbo had no difficulty in stomaching his comment.

'But what about the rest of the book . . . don't you find Bergman enormously self-obsessed? He's got a stomach-ache the whole way through the book, hasn't he?'

I really tried to get Garbo going.

'He's quite right, Ingmar Bergman. That's what life is like. And as for me, there's hardly been a single day in the whole of my life when I have felt completely well. The only thing that was odd about Bergman was that he used to laugh a bit hysterically. He had an ugly laugh.

'When I visited Bergman in Råsunda he gave me a present, a mascot: a little bear made of wood that one of his children had carved. That is the best present I ever received.'

Whenever Garbo vanished into the kitchen, I took the opportunity to look at another book she was reading: a guide to positive thinking. Garbo had obviously taken the book's message to heart and was trying to see the world through positive eyes. Indeed I was very impressed by Garbo's independence. She proved she did the most essential things herself.

Previously in Klosters Garbo had mentioned an Ingmar Bergman film, *Såsom i en spegel*. That was the best film she had ever seen. I had asked her then what especially had fascinated her. She had said, '*Mirror*, as the film is called in English, is the truest film I have ever seen. Life is just like that. I have seen the film twice in New York. And I'd like to see it again. I would be very grateful, Mr Broman, if you could help to arrange for me to see it.'

I had been more than happy to do so. I got in touch with the Museum of Modern Art in New York by telephone from Stockholm. It was easy to arrange the showing of the, film. I spoke to a Mr Charles Silver, a very kind gentleman. When I told him that Greta Garbo wanted to see the film, they were keen to roll out the welcome mat.

I told her this, that the showing had now been arranged. She thanked me but said that she was not up to it at the moment. It would have to be another time.

Mirror is in part an attempt to give shape and substance to the problems of the artist's search for truth, of his relationship with his audience, and of artistic failure and superficial success.

I had never succeeded in getting Garbo to develop her own thoughts on these questions, which is why I had been so looking forward to going with her to see the film.

From the little Garbo said I understood that Ingmar Bergman had given artistic form to a problem that had been preoccupying her for a long time: that of the artist who compromises his art in order to captivate the rest of the world and in doing so risks losing himself

Before we left, Garbo showed us a small part of the apartment. She told us that they had been having problems with the pipes throughout the building and she had been plagued by all the consequences. Much worse though had been a burglary three years ago when she had been away. The thieves had got into several apartments—with false keys. The things they had stolen from Garbo's apartment included a silver tray and a silver bowl she had been given by the Count and Countess Wachtmeister at Tistad. She missed them very much.

The next morning Garbo rang at nine-thirty. She was in a good mood and was kind enough to say that she thought my wife and I suited one another so well.

She returned to our discussion about Ingmar Bergman. 'But Mr Broman, we shouldn't be too critical, we should be understanding.'

Garbo was busy the rest of that week, but she telephoned every morning and was very chatty. Now and again she would touch on things she was reading and would without any prompting recite poetry on the telephone. One morning she read a poem by Heinrich Heine, one of her favourites. An English prose translation of the Swedish version she recited reads as follows:

Fortune's a wanton who never stays for long and her favour does not last. She smoothes your hair back from your forehead, kisses you quickly and flits away.

But Lady Sorrow takes you in her heavy heart for days and nights on end. She is in no hurry. She sits down by your bed and does her knitting.

Garbo's 'kidney-doctor' was a regular visitor. Garbo complained that she could not help with exercising her legs—she did not want anything to do with the exercise bike I suggested.

Then she wondered if we would be visiting Klosters in summer. She wanted to make sure of our company. She told us she had been warned not to walk alone on solitary paths. 'If anything happened, I might just lie there and die in the end . . .'

17

'If You Want To See A Star, Look At Me'

It was well known in Hollywood that Garbo found it easy to learn things by heart. Maybe this was why she liked reciting poetry. What happened any number of times in Klosters was that she would suddenly start reciting a poem she knew by heart.

Året Runt once published a letter from a subscriber in Denver, Colorado, Eric W. Stromqvist:

In the course of a year in Hollywood at the beginning of the thirties, I came into contact of a sort with Greta Garbo. I was an electrician and used to work at MGM's film studios. She told me that her favourite poet just then was the Persian poet Omar Khayyam. A verse she once read to me went like this:

Ah, fill the cup what—boots it to repeat
How time is slipping underneath our
   feet:
Unborn tomorrow and dead yesterday
Why fret about them if today be sweet?

This calls to mind an occasion in the thirties when Garbo was spending Christmas in Sweden and Louis B. Mayer & Co. were waiting for a decision from her. She only sent a single Christmas greeting by telegram to MGM—to her favourite cameraman, William Daniels. She also asked him to wish a happy Christmas to 'the riggers, the set-workers and the electricians'—to the people who did the hard work on her films.

In Klosters Garbo told me that she always tried to defend the writers whenever their fates were being discussed by Louis B. Mayer or his closest associates:

'You can't imagine how ignorant he was, that Mr Mayer. Once he said to Louis B. Bromfield, straight to the writer's face: "Mr Bromberg, we're not interested in your script or your treatment—we're only interested in your name."'

'Which reminds me,' said Garbo, 'of what Mr Samuel Goldwyn said during a

270

discussion about a theatre play they were considering filming in which a woman was said to be a lesbian. They did not know who to use to fill the role: "That's no problem. If we can't find anyone from Lesbia, we'll get someone from Bulgaria or Rumania" '

And he wasn't joking.

As mentioned earlier, Harriet Löwenhjelm became one of Garbo's favourite poets very early on. One evening when she was in the mood she sang the beginning of 'Beatrice Aurore':

In the Old Town, by Kornhamnstorg,
at Hallbeck's second-hand bookshop
I bought an old book of dreams
in folio

Garbo's most cherished poem was also by Harriet Löwenhjelm and when she used to read it brought tears to your eyes:

The children of this world go dancing
   now,
treading the boards of vanity,
but I wind the yarn of dreams
alone with the roses and the lily.

The children of the world bill and coo
they preen themselves and go a-
　　wooing
but I play my own game
alone with the rose and the lily

I never did see my own true love
save only in my dreams
Green was the dress she wore
green with rosy seams

We gave Garbo Harriet Löwenhjelm's collected poems, which pleased her very much. But I suspect that she already had several copies.

A Swedish classic that Garbo recited to us was by Victor Rydberg—she knew two verses of 'Tomten' ('Puck') by heart. When we sent her an anthology that included the text of 'Tomten' we were all surprised at how many verses there actually are in this poem.

When I saw the address labels on Garbo's suitcases in her hotel room with the name Harriet Brown I could not help asking if it was Harriet Löwenhjelm's name she had had in mind.

'Yes, you're quite right. I thought Harriet was a beautiful name . . .'

'But what about Brown, was that for Clarence Brown, the film cameraman.'

'No, not at all. I really did like Mr Brown, but I chose Brown because it is such a common name in America. I wanted something that would not call attention to itself. But over the years I have had a variety of invented names on my suitcases and they have sadly always been seen through. The same thing still applies today. I can't use my own name, because then people would just take things that belong to me. That applies to letters as well, letters to me that have gone adrift.'

Writers constituted a group of people Garbo particularly cared about. That affection seams to have been mutual. Louis B. Bromfield visited Sweden at the beginning of the thirties and was interviewed in *Vecko-Journalen* (a weekly magazine):

'I have met Garbo a great many times in Hollywood. But the first time I saw her I felt I had had an extraordinary experience—one of those great experiences that you only have once or twice in a lifetime.

'It sounds sentimental to say this, but there is something unearthly about her. Not that she seems too good for this world or that she is not made of flesh and blood like the rest of us.

'I think I can best express what I mean when I say that she is universal. Just like everyone else and not like anyone. And then, she is very natural. There is not the least little bit of affectation in her personality. Her great success as an actress in films is based on that one thing, that she has learnt to be wholly and fully herself.

'Shy? No, Garbo is not shy. I have never seen anyone who seemed to be so unperturbed.'

In the summer of 1938 Garbo drove with Nils and Hörke Wachtmeister over to Norway and they were invited to dinner at the Fritzöhus, at Larvik, outside Oslo. Their host was the owner of the estate, Fritz Mikael Treschow. Notable among the guests was the Norwegian poet, Herman Wildenvey, who wrote a lyrical article about Garbo immediately after meeting her:

'Garbo was a bit worried that she might not understand Norwegian. Nils Wachtmeister had just been telling a story about Ole Bull [the Norwegian musician whose compositions include 'Säterjäntans söndag' ('Säter-Girl's Sunday') who was once a guest of Frederik II of Denmark. The

King had asked him how he had learnt to play.

' "It was Norway's fjords, Norway's mountains and her foaming waterfalls that taught me, Your Majesty," said Ole Bull.

' "*Sikke noe vrövl* [Stuff and nonsense]," the King said.

'Greta Garbo thought the story was priceless and practised saying "*Sikke noe vrövl*".

' "But that's Danish," Wachtmeister said.

' "Yes but the foaming waterfalls were Norwegian," said Garbo. For she had enjoyed the wonderful trip in an open car through Norway and seen many a foaming waterfall.'

Wildenvey was asked to read some of his own love poems. He stared fixedly at Garbo and according to some reports could never stop reading. When Wildenvey was rung up by a newspaper the next day, he summed up his impression of Garbo thus: 'She is enchanting—a natural wonder and a child of nature.'

The French Nobel laureate, François Mauriac, wrote an essay, 'An Evening with Greta Garbo', which was translated into Swedish by Stig Ahlgren:

'A weak and feverish youth, lost in the endless sea of humanity, has to ride out on his own the immense storm of the senses unleashed by Greta Garbo's wonderful eyes. There is no desire that is not awakened by this being who is at once real and intangible. With impunity she can smile, part her lips, raise and lower her bosom. There she is as large as life, offering herself to millions of men.'

Garbo has also been praised here in Sweden. In 1964 Olof Lagercrantz wrote in *Dagens Nyheter:*

'It is impossible to know whether Greta Garbo herself knows what she is doing in her acting. She has been called mysterious and her life has been a mysterious one. Why did she retire so early? Is it because she knew that her theme was that of the pilgrim, and that her pure, cool, divine beauty was the necessary precondition of that theme and that that beauty would only belong to her for a few short years?

'Beauty has fallen into disrepute, because in this age of ours it is so often connected with that which is erotically attractive, charming and striking.'

Brigit Tengroth wrote in 1959 about the time when as a girl she saw the première of the silent version of *Anna Karenina (Love)*:

'*Anna Karenina* is my favourite book and Tolstoy my favourite author.

'What I can remember from that time is how the auditorium darkened to a magical Chagall blue, and from the film itself the scene in which Anna Karenina stole in to see her little son, whom she had abandoned, and how the dark stains of anguish blossomed at the armholes of her dress. As I was a child I liked that scene the best. I could never forget Garbo's translucent, marked face. Where did that light come from and how could suffering be beautiful?

'Children cannot help being merciless critics. They only remember what was good, the bad sinks into oblivion. Those critics who advise us to forget Garbo's face for Anna Karenina's do not know what they are talking about. They have not read their Tolstoy.

'Garbo did not need to read Tolstoy and pull faces in front of the dressing-room mirror, she had been given that face as a gift.'

In 1947 Gerd Kibbing wrote in *Dagens Nyheter,* having seen *Camille:*

'Well, what *I* will be telling my children and grandchildren about, is what I have only been able to experience through Garbo— that her very face is a work of drama, that it can reflect feelings and sensations to such an intense degree that you are unable to analyze them. You are just carried away, in the grip of a tension that is much greater than that in thrillers and which makes you gasp for breath. It is impossible to describe. When we left the cinema, people were going home as though they had been to mass. That is the power of the personality.'

As far as I know Garbo would have read all these articles. She had good friends who sent her newspaper cuttings and she saw to it that she was kept abreast of most of what was written about her in Sweden. By way of contrast I would like to quote Berndt Carlberg, one of the busiest composers of comic songs we have ever had in Sweden:

'It was the spring of 1929. I was staying at the Grand Hotel in Saltsjöbaden in order to write some lyrics for Ernst Rolf. The really important ones were for that charming tune "Wenn der weisse Flieder wieder blüht".

'I was lying in bed in the early morning and humming away at it, trying to find inspiration. Hjalmar Bergman was staying in the room above me and used to talk on the telephone with the mighty sound of an organ trumpet. I suddenly heard him mention Garbo's name.

'I opened the day's edition of the paper and read what I supposed Bergman had been reading, namely that Garbo who just then was visiting home had sat as a model in the foyer of the Palladium for a group of young artists. There it was—all laid out for me, the idea for the performance by the star of the revue, Margit Rosengren. I sketched out the scene itself and the arrangement and went for a walk. An hour later I came back and had the text already finished in my head:

Woman, woman, woman, she used just to
  be a poem.
I want to show you woman as a modern
  problem.
You young people who have been hunting
  high and low
for a woman who is very special
turn the radiator in your hearts to cold
and start drawing, for I am a model.

If you want to see a star, look at me.
You are most welcome to look at me.
I can cry tears,
I can shoot thunderbolts
I am the Primadonna Assoluta.
I am the industry's latest fad, look at me.
I am the new fashion-plate, look at me.
Everything is done in the USA to captivate
  the world
If you want to see a Muse, look at me.

Margit Rosengren fell ill after the première and Ernst Rolf had to find a replacement for her. He found one in Norrköping where an unknown beginner, Zarah Leander, came to sing at an audition for Rolf. She was immediately taken on and made her debut with 'If you want to see a star' when the Rolf revue came to Borås in August 1929. Zarah was dressed and made up to look like Garbo and got fifteen kronor a day.

As we all know, this comic song came to be Zarah's theme tune. Eventually people forgot that the song was about Garbo.

When I reminded Garbo about the song, she remembered it very well—I could see that. But what she said, rather modestly, was: 'Was that song really about me? She really did sing very well, Zarah Leander, didn't she? I liked her.'

Whenever we discussed writers with Garbo, she would perk up and become more talkative than usual. She asked me if I had read an American book that had a large section devoted to Garbo in literature, published by a university in Pittsburgh. No, I had not heard of it. A few days later Garbo turned up the name of the book and I had it sent from England.

The author, whose name was Bernard Bergonzi, wrote about the thirties. One chapter dealt with the references to and use of Garbo in literature, ranging from hit tunes to the novels of Graham Greene. According to Bergonzi, out of all the Hollywood stars, Garbo was the one who was named most often in every possible kind of literary context.

In a song by Cole Porter there are the words:

Is it Maurice's hat
or a furnished flat
that makes your pulses beat?
Is your paradise
In Garbo's eyes
Or Ginger Rogers' feet?

Again, these lines come from 'These Foolish Things' by Strachey, Link and Marvell:

The smile of Garbo and the scent of roses, the waiter's whistle as the last bar closes.

In another song by Cole Porter, 'You're the Top,' we have:

You're the National Gallery
You're Garbo's salary . . .

Evelyn Waugh was a frequent cinemagoer. In *Vile Bodies* he has a couple of his main characters discuss Garbo.

George Orwell uses Garbo to brighten up one of his novels—*Keep the Aspidistra Flying*.

One of the main characters in Lawrence Durrell's *The Black Book* refers to the 'Swedish man-eater, Greta Garbo'.

Barbara Lucas has a description of Garbo in her novel *Stars Were Born*. And in Anthony Powell's *Agents and Patients* Garbo is included in the description of Berlin.

Garbo is mentioned in two novels by Graham Greene: *Brighton Rock* and *England Made Me*.

Roland Barthes wrote an essay in 1950 about Garbo, which he based on her beauty as Queen Christina:

'Garbo offered us a sort of Platonic idea of beauty in human form, which explains why her face is sexually indefinable although you are never left in any doubt.'

Further on he states:

'Garbo's face is an idea, while its opposite is the face of Audrey Hepburn, which is an event.

I used to speak with Garbo on the phone off and on. I remember that she once suddenly started associating something we were discussing with a piece of poetry. And then she started reciting a poem by Heinrich Heine that she knew by heart.

The year 1985 saw Garbo's eightieth birthday and the centenary of Blekinge Street. Stig Claesson wrote about the occasion in the evening paper *Aftonbladet:*

'I know that celebrities like the sports commentator, Bengt Grive, will be hugely pleased. That's where he comes from. That is as it should be. On the bottom floor of the building on Blekinge Street that now houses the Pelican restaurant, there used to be what was known as a ping-pong hall. This was a cellar in which you could play table-tennis. It was a large, smoky, and very unhealthy place usually known as Vålådalen. And Grive knew how to play table-tennis. And he still does if you ask him. I think that Vålådalen was, if not owned, at least run by Björn Borg's father, which would mean that Björn Borg was born on Blekinge Street.

'And who should be more pleased than Greta Garbo? . . .

'. . . But let us all throughout the whole of Södermalm [Stockholm's South Island] sing the praises of Greta Garbo.

The building she lived in—we tore it
   down.
What shall we build for her?
She has made herself immortal.

'There is one sense though in which Bengt Grive is right to be the cockiest. He grew up on a street that has been made immortal by an ordinary Miss Gustafsson.'

Let Erik Lindorm (1935) round off this cavalcade:

'Garbo is the world's best known and least known actress, the most photographed recluse in the world. The Swedish lass, who wishes to remain unnoticed, is the most noticed film star in the world. And the more noticed she is, the more unnoticed she deserves to be. And the more she tries to pass unnoticed, the more noticed she gets.'

18

The Real Garbo

The question I get asked most often is: 'What was Garbo *really* like?'

I have tried to record my impressions as straightforwardly as possible. There were times when Garbo could appear to be *both* shy and self-confident. She was unpredictable.

The first thing that struck me was the beauty of her voice. It was so well preserved, so sonorous. And she spoke such lovely Swedish, without any accent, though she was happier with weights and measures in American and she knew nothing of the latest slang words in Swedish. When we went on a shopping expedition to Davos and I said in Swedish 'what a chic dress', she asked what the Swedish slang-word for 'chic' meant; was it something to do with chick-peas?

She had a rich vocabulary and found it easy to hit on just the right expression—

'There are more swear-words in Swedish than in American English.' Quite simply, she had a good ear for language.

Garbo still had her classic profile. Naturally her brow and her nose and cheeks aged, but they were well preserved. Old people's eyes normally get smaller with the passing of the years. But not Garbo's. Her eyes were still large and deep. It was her chin that was wrinkled and there were wrinkles around her mouth as well. Her eyelashes were long, although not as long as in the good old days. Now and then she would wear mascara in the evening.

She wore lipstick and would make up when we were out in the evening.

Her hair was greyish-white and would later become a bit too long.

'They've offered to cut my hair here at the hotel, but I don't want to. I could also cut my own hair—not that I'd get round to it.'

Unfortunately, she was inflexible on that point. Otherwise her hair was in good condition and well looked after.

Garbo's posture when seated was always very free and easy. She had a long, straight back. She walked with a slight forward stoop and before she hurt her leg and foot, she used her walking-stick more for company than support.

Compared with many people of the same age, Garbo maintained a youthful image. She was relaxed and easygoing, with a cultivated and worldly manner.

She had rather small, well-cared-for hands. The only jewellery she wore was a gold signet ring on the ring-finger of her left hand. She had a large gold wristwatch with a rather wide gold bracelet—no little lady's watch for her. She never wore earrings in our company, never a necklace, never a brooch—just that one ring on her left hand. She would sometimes sit there swinging her ring about while talking and I was curious as to what it represented but was unwilling to ask.

I mentioned our admiring the ring to Gunnila Bernadotte, who immediately supplied the answer:

'That was the Wachtmeister family ring she was wearing. She had already been given it as a memento of my mother and father in the thirties.'

So it was Nils and Hörke who had given her the ring as a token of their close friendship. It was worn but you could just make out the Wachtmeister crest that adorned it:

three stars, a sabre and a crane's foot, standing for: eternity, strength and knowledge.

Garbo was wearing the ring when she died.

I can remember Garbo sighing: 'I would have liked to be a countess.'

I do not think you should read too much into these words. But we may safely conclude that Garbo's relations with the Wachtmeister family and the castle at Tistad were harmonious, like the whole of that setting and atmosphere that had been such a refuge for her when fleeing the nervous tension of Hollywood.

Why then did she give up making films, apparently so contrarily? A vital part of the answer can be found in Garbo's letters to Hörke from Hollywood. In these she talked about her health problems, and her consequent ambition to amass sufficient earnings to secure her future and make herself economically independent.

Then the war intervened. For the six years between 1939 and 1945 she did not feel she could cross the Atlantic and so go home to Sweden.

Garbo's lack of self-confidence was also of great significance in determining the final outcome. It may seem incomprehensible to most of us, with all the extraordinary success that she had, that she could feel so little faith in herself. Perhaps this should not be exaggerated, but her hesitancy and inability to make up her mind were also part of the whole complex.

She was also a realist and that had a part to play as well: she realized that she had lived the high life on her youth and beauty—and that they were qualities that would fade with time.

Garbo was an intelligent and cautious strategist. In 1946 when she returned to New York from her first trip to Sweden for many years, she was met by a horde of journalists:

'I have made no plans, neither for films nor for anything else. I am just flowing with the current,' she said.

Garbo was something of a perfectionist. What emerged from a number of conversations was that when she was filming and making her preparations she gave herself over to this—completely. Nothing was allowed to disturb her. She concentrated totally on the task in hand.

There can be no doubt that Garbo was fully aware that her trump card was her youth and beauty. She did not have a complex about growing old but she did not want to spoil her image for the cinema audience.

Garbo was timeless. When you take a second look at her earliest films, the other actors come across as very dated, not least the men. Nowadays there is something slightly ridiculous about them all. But not Garbo.

The film cameramen knew very well that Garbo's face was perfect from every angle. Many great stars favour a particular profile, some the left profile, some the right. There could on occasion be a problem when two stars were supposed to kiss in close-up when they both favoured their left profiles. Garbo was above worries of this kind.

I told her that Norman Mailer, the writer, having written a book about Marilyn Monroe and now a man of mature years, had become a Garbo worshipper. I heard this from Lars Forssell, a member of the Swedish Academy, who had met Mailer in New York. Mailer went to see every Garbo film that came his way. He had come to realize that Garbo was the most beautiful and the greatest and the most intelligent actress of them all.

'Then I had better keep out of the way

291

so that he can maintain the illusion. If he saw me in reality he would definitely stop going to the cinema.'

Garbo seemed to us to be an unsentimental and matter-of-fact person. She was truthful and honest in the best sense of the word.

Of course, she was an actress—she was very aware of the fact that it was Greta Garbo' sitting there. As soon as a curious passer-by would linger near our table she had an ability to look through that person as though they were thin air.

I think she grew reconciled to her life as she got older. There was no bitterness in the Garbo we met, even though she might have been unhappy about some of the things in her past. She appeared to be growing old gracefully.

Talking about growing old: on one occasion when we were discussing Selma Lagerlöf—who it turns out is the Swedish writer whose work has been filmed the most—Garbo asked me how old she was when she died. She was eighty, I replied.

'But eighty is no age at all!' Garbo said.

This was quite true in the case of Greta Garbo.

All the recognition and honours pleased

her greatly, they helped to improve her self-confidence.

'Moje knew how to encourage insecure people,' escaped her lips on several occasions.

Joe Lombardo, Garbo's old friend in New York, rang one day and asked me to ring Garbo. She had tried to reach our number in Stockholm without success. Her health was poor. She was lying in bed. But she wanted me to pass on her thanks to the minister of finance, Kjell-Olof Feldt, for the lovely gift made to her by the Swedish government, of a crystal vase from Orrefors bearing the Swedish national coat of arms:

'To think that you all remember me in Sweden. That makes me so happy. The crystal vase is so huge I could have a bath in it . . .

Feldt and Birgitta von Otter had taken the vase with them on a trip to New York.

When the Swedish king and queen were in the USA for the Delaware Jubileum, an informal meeting was successfully arranged with Garbo in New York at the home of Gilbert Kaplan and his wife Lena, who is the daughter of Professor Gunnar Björck.

I rang Garbo as soon as I heard the news on the radio. She was obviously thrilled and delighted about meeting them:

'I was kidnapped. They came by car to pick me up. All I had to do was get in, although it was about twenty years too late for it all. Queen Silvia was quite marvellous—we really do have the most beautiful queen in the world. But Mr Broman, I must tell you that I did something very silly: I wore my dark glasses, which may have meant the king couldn't see what I looked like . . . I met his father, you know, Prince Gustav Adolf.'

The royal couple had presented Garbo with a photograph of themselves.

However, my picture of Garbo would be a distorted one if she were seen only surrounded by kings and queens, Churchill and Onassis, and the like.

In 1925, as the nineteen-year-old Garbo was finishing work on the film *Die Freudlose Strasse* (The Joyless Street) in Berlin, the film company asked her what she would like to do on the last evening. Her hosts were keen on staging a banquet or something of that kind. But Garbo said immediately: 'I want to go to Luna Park.'

This was the funfair in Berlin; and that is where they went. Garbo went on the roller-coaster fifteen times. She never tired of going on the roundabout or of shooting at the bull's eye.

The same thing happened in Santa Monica when Garbo was first in Hollywood: there was a fairground near her hotel that she used to visit in secret.

When Garbo visited Stockholm for the last time in 1962, she told Mimi Pollak that she had just received a telegram at the Grand Hotel, where she was staying, from George Schlee, who had been her companion for a couple of decades. Schlee informed Garbo that he could not marry her: his wife (Valentina, the dress designer) refused to give him a divorce because she was a Catholic. Schlee died in 1964.

Several of the Swedes I have spoken to who met Schlee found it difficult to understand what Garbo saw in him. They did not like him.

A couple of Americans I have spoken with hold the opposite view. Schlee was a Jew and was reputed to be phenomenal at telling funny stories, particularly Jewish jokes. He was a one-man show. Garbo had fun with him.

Several of her letters to Hörke she signed 'The Clown'. This was another side to her personality.

Garbo stayed away from Klosters for the summer of 1989. She was too ill and too weak to travel. She was affected by chronic bronchitis, emphysema, problems with her circulation, the difficulties she had in walking as a consequence of hurting her foot and most of all by her kidney disease, which required her to undergo dialysis three times a week.

But Garbo was still bright and cheerful when I spoke to her on the phone. She had got a new home help. The new woman, to whom I had only talked on the telephone, was from Haiti and had a strong French accent:

'You must remember, Mr Broman, that Mrs [!] Garbo is at the hospital on Mondays, Wednesdays and Fridays [for dialysis] so you will have to ring later.'

A week before Garbo's death, my wife and I were in New York on our way to Florida. Garbo sounded bright and friendly as usual, but I could hear that she was very weak. She still managed to comment on the shipping accident between Norway and Denmark a few days earlier, in which so many people had died. She was appalled that that kind of thing could happen.

Garbo made a note of my room number at the hotel and promised to ring when she felt better. That was on the Sunday evening.

Three days later, on the Wednesday, she was taken to New York Hospital by ambulance. She died at the hospital after another three days—on 15 April 1990—at the age of eighty-four years and seven months.

The Films Of Greta Garbo

Silent Films

TITLE   ***Luffar-Peter (Peter the Tramp)***

Direction   Erik A. Petschler
Script   Erik A. Petschler
Photography   Oscar Norberg
Production   Petscher-Film
Première   26 December 1922
Starring   Erik A. Petschler, Gucken Cederborg, Tyra Ryman, Greta Gustaffson

TITLE   ***Gösta Berlings Saga (The Story of Gösta Berling)***

Direction   Mauritz Stiller
Script   Mauritz Stiller/Ragnar HylténCavallius; based on the novel by

	Selma Lagerlöf
Photography	Julius Jaenzon
Production	Svensk Filmindustri
Première	10 March 1924 (Part I); 17 March 1924 (Part II)
Starring	Lars Hansson Gerda Lundequist, Greta Garbo, Mona Mårtensson, Otto Elg-Lundberg, Sixten Malmerfeldt, Karin Swanström, Ellen Cederström, Jenny Hasselqvist, Torsten Harmmarén, Svend Kornbeck, Sven Scholander, Knut Lambert, Hugo Rönnblad, Gaston Portefaix, Albert Ståhl

TITLE	***Die Freudlose Gasse (The Joyless Street)***
Direction	Georg Wilhelm Pabst
Script	Willi Haas/G. W. Pabst; based on a novel by Hugo Bettauer
Photography	Guido Seeber, Curt Oertel, Walter Robert Lach
Production	Hirschel-Solar-Film,

	Berlin
Première	18 May 1925
Starring	Werner Krauss, Asta Nielsen, Greta Garbo, Jaro Fürth, Einar Hanson, Karl Ettlinger

All the rest of Garbo's films were produced by Metro-Goldwyn-Mayer in the USA:

TITLE	***The Torrent***
Direction	Monta Bell
Script	Dorothy Farnum; based on a novel by Vicente Blasco-Ibáñez, *Entre Naranjos*
Photography	William Daniels
Première	21 February 1926
Starring	Ricardo Cortez, Greta Garbo, Gertrude Olmsted

TITLE	***The Temptress***
Direction	Mauritz Stiller and Fred Niblo
Script	Dorothy Famum; based on a novel by Vicente Blasco-Ibáñez, *La Terra de Todos*

Photography	Tony Gaudio
Première	10 October 1926
Starring	Antonio Moreno, Greta Garbo, Roy D'Arcy, Marc McDermott, Lionel Barrymore

TITLE	*Flesh and the Devil*
Direction	Clarence Brown
Script	Benjanain Glazer; based on a novel by Herman Sudermann, *Es war*
Photography	William Daniels
Première	9 January 1927
Starring	John Gilbert, Greta Garbo, Lars Hanson

TITLE	*Love* (in Sweden this film was known as *Anna Karenina,* like the later sound film)
Direction	Edmund Goulding
Script	Francis Marion; based on the novel by Leo Tolstoy, *Anna Karenina*
Photography	William Daniels
Première	29 November 1927
Starring	Greta Garbo, John Gilbert, George Fawcett

TITLE	***The Divine Woman***
Direction	Victor Sjöström
Script	Dorothy Farnum; based on a play by Gladys Unger, *Starlight*
Photography	Oliver Marsh
Première	14 January 1928
Starring	Greta Garbo, Lars Hanson, Lowell Sherman, Polly Moran

TITLE	***The Mysterious Lady***
Direction	Fred Niblo
Script	Bess Meredyth; based on a novel by Ludwig Wolff, *Krieg im Dunkel*
Photography	William Daniels
Première	4 August 1928
Starring	Greta Garbo, Conrad Nagel, Gustav von Seyffertitz

TITLE	***A Woman of Affairs***
Direction	Clarence Brown
Script	Bess Meredyth; based on a novel by Michael Arlen, *The Green Hat*
Photography	William Daniels
Première	19 January 1929

Starring	Greta Garbo, John Gilbert, Lewis Stone, Douglas Fairbanks Jr.
TITLE	***Wild Orchids***
Direction	Sidney Franklin
Script	Hans Kraly, Richard Shayer and Willis Goldbeck; based on a novel by John Colton, *Heat*
Photography	William Daniels
Première	30 March 1929
Starting	Greta Garbo, Lewis Stone, Nils Asther
TITLE	***The Single Standard***
Direction	John S. Robertson
Script	Josephine Lovett; based on the novel by Adela Rogers St John
Photography	Oliver Marsh
Première	27 July 1929
Starting	Greta Garbo, Nils Asther, John Mack Brown
TITLE	***The Kiss***
Direction	Jacques Feyder
Script	Hans Kraly; based on a

	film idea by George M. Saville
Photography	William Daniels
Première	15 November 1929
Starting	Greta Garbo, Conrad Nagel

Sound Films

TITLE	*Anna Christie*
Direction	Clarence Brown
Script	Frances Marion; based on the play by Eugene O'Neill
Photography	William Daniels
Première	14 March 1930
Starring	Greta Garbo, Charles Bickford, Marie Dressier
TITLE	*Romance*
Direction	Clarence Brown
Script	Bess Meredyth and Edwin Justus Mayer; based on Edward Sheldon's play *Signora Vallini*
Photography	William Daniels
Première	22 August 1930
Starring	Greta Garbo, Lewis Stone, Gavin Gordon, Elliott Nugent
TITLE	*Inspiration*
Direction	Clarence Brown

305

Script	Gene Markey
Photography	William Daniels
Première	6 February 1931
Starring	Greta Garbo, Robert Montgomery, Lewis Stone, Marjorie Rambeau

TITLE	***Susan Lenox: Her Fall and Rise***
Direction	Robert Z. Leonard
Script	Wanda Tuchock; based on a novel by David Graham Phillips, *Susan Lenox*
Photography	William Daniels
Première	16 October 1931
Starring	Greta Garbo, Clark Gable, Jean Hersholt, John Miljan

TITLE	***Mata Hari***
Direction	George Fitzmaurice
Script	Benjamin Glazer and Leo Birinski
Photography	William Daniels
Première	31 October 1931
Starring	Greta Garbo, Ramon Novarro, Lionel Barry-

more, Lewis Stone

TITLE	**Grand Hotel**
Direction	Edmund Goulding
Script	William A. Drake; based on a novel and play by Vicki Baum, *Menschen im Hotel*
Photography	William Daniels
Première	12 April 1932
Starring	Greta Garbo, John Barrymore, Joan Crawford, Lionel Barrymore, Lewis Stone, Jean Hersholt, Wallace Beery

TITLE	**As You Desire Me**
Direction	George Fitzmaurice
Script	Gene Markey; based on a play by Luigi Pirandello, *Come tu mi vuoi*
Photography	William Daniels
Première	2 June 1932
Starring	Greta Garbo, Melvyn Douglas, Erich von Stroheim, Owen Moore, Hedda Hopper

TITLE	**Queen Christina**

Direction	Rouben Mamoulian
Script	Salka Viertel and H. M. Harwood; based on an idea by Salka Viertel and Margaret F. Levine
Photography	William Daniels
Première	26 December 1933
Starring	Greta Garbo, John Gilbert, Ian Keith, Lewis Stone

TITLE	*The Painted Veil*
Direction	Richard Boleslawski
Script	John Meehan, Salka Viertel and Edith Fitzgerald; based on the novel by Somerset Maugham
Photography	William Daniels
Première	7 October 1934
Starring	Greta Garbo, Herbert Marshall, George Brent, Wamer Oland, Jean Hersholt

TITLE	*Anna Karenina*
Direction	Clarence Brown
Script	Clemence Dane and Salka Viertel; based on

	the novel by Leo Tolstoy
Photography	William Daniels
Première	30 August 1935
Starring	Greta Garbo, Fredric March, May Robson, Freddie Bartholomew, Maureen O'Sullivan, Basil Rathbone, Reginald Owen, Reginald Denny

TITLE	*Camille*
Direction	George Cukor
Script	Zoe Atkins, Frances Marion and James Hilton; based on the novel and play by Alexandre Dumas fils, *La Dame aux Camélias*
Photography	William Daniels
Première	22 January 1937
Starring	Greta Garbo, Robert Taylor, Lionel Barrymore

TITLE	*Conquest*
Direction	Clarence Brown
Script	Samuel Hoffenstein, Salka Viertel and S. N.

309

	Behrman; based on the novel by Waclaw Gasiorowski, *Pani Waleska*
Photography	Karl Freund
Première	4 November 1937
Starring	Greta Garbo, Charles Boyer, Reginald Owen

TITLE	*Ninotchka*
Direction	Ernst Lubitsch
Script	Charles Brackett, Billy Wilder and Walter Reisch; based on an idea by Melchior Lengyel
Photography	William Daniels
Première	9 November 1939
Starring	Greta Garbo, Melvyn Douglas, Ina Claire, Bela Lugosi

TITLE	*Two-Faced Woman*
Direction	George Cukor
Script	S. N. Berhman, Salka Viertel and George Oppenheimer; based on the play by Ludwig Fulda
Photography	Joseph Ruttenberg

Première	31 December 1941
Starring	Greta Garbo, Melvyn Douglas, Constance Bennett, Roland Young, Robert Sterling, Ruth Gordon

ISIS LARGE PRINT

ISIS publish a wide range of books in large print, from fiction to biography. A full list of titles is available free of charge from the address below. Alternatively, contact your local library for details of their collection of ISIS books.

Details of ISIS unabridged audio books are also available.

Any suggestions for books you would like to see in large print or audio are always welcome.

ISIS
55 St Thomas' Street
Oxford OX1 1JG
(0865) 250333